PAUL GASCOIGNE
EIGHT

PAUL GASCOIGNE
EIGHT

RS

Reach Sport

Reach **Sport**

w w w . r e a c h s p o r t . c o m

1

Written with Victoria Williams

Published in Great Britain and Ireland in 2025 by Reach Sport.

www.reachsport.com
@Reach_Sport

Reach Sport is a part of Reach PLC.

Hardback ISBN: 9781916811430
eBook ISBN: 9781916811447
Trade Paperback ISBN: 9781916811454

Photographic acknowledgements:
Paul Gascoigne personal collection, Mirrorpix, Alamy.

Every effort has been made to trace the copyright.
Any oversight will be rectified in future editions.

Editor: Simon Monk
Production: Christine Costello
Cover Design: Chris Collins

Printed and bound by CPI Group (UK) Ltd,
Croydon, CR0 4YY.

FSC
www.fsc.org

MIX
Paper | Supporting
responsible forestry
FSC® C013604

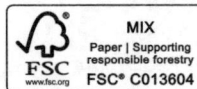

CONTENTS

TIMELINE

PAUL JOHN GASCOIGNE

1967

May 27th, born in family home on Rose Street, Teams, Gateshead, to John and Carol Gascoigne

1980

Newcastle United schoolboy apprentice

1983

Newcastle United youth apprentice

1985

April 13th, Newcastle United first team debut v QPR
May 10th, FA Youth Cup final victory v Watford
May, Newcastle United professional contract
Newcastle United 1984/85 season: 2 appearances, 0 goals
September 21st, first goal for Newcastle United v Oxford United

1986

Newcastle United 1985/86 season: 35 appearances, 9 goals
July, makes front cover of Rothman's Football Yearbook

1987

Newcastle United 1986/87 season: 27 appearances, 5 goals
June 7th, England U21 debut v Morocco

1988

April, PFA Young Player of the Year 1987/88
Newcastle United 1987/88 season: 43 appearances, 11 goals
July, transfer to Tottenham Hotspur £2.2m
September 14th, England senior debut v Denmark

1989

April 26th, first England goal v Albania
Tottenham Hotspur 1988/89 season: 37 appearances, 7 goals

1990

Tottenham Hotspur 1989/90 season: 38 appearances, 7 goals
June-July, Italia '90 World Cup
November, "Fog on the Tyne (Revisited)" by Gazza and
Lindisfarne reaches Number 2 in the UK Charts
December, BBC Sports Personality of the Year

1991

May 18th, FA Cup Final victory v Nottingham Forest
Tottenham Hotspur 1990/91 season: 37 appearances, 19 goals

1992

May, transfer to Lazio £5.5m
September 27th, Lazio debut v Genoa

1993

Lazio 1992/93 season: 26 appearances, 4 goals

1994

Lazio 1993/94 season: 17 appearances, 2 goals

1995

Lazio 1994/95 season: 4 appearances, 0 goals
July, transfer to Rangers £4.3m

1996

February 18th, birth of Regan Paul Gascoigne
May, Scottish Premier Division victory
May 18th, Scottish Cup victory v Hearts
May, SWFA Footballer of the Year
May, PFA Scotland Players' Player of the Year
Rangers 1995/96 season: 42 appearances, 19 goals
June, Euro '96 European Championship
July 1st, wedding to Sheryl Failes
November 24th, Scottish League Cup victory v Hearts

1997

May, Scottish Premier Division victory
Rangers 1996/97 season: 34 appearances, 17 goals

1998

Rangers 1997/98 season: 28 appearances, 3 goals
March, transfer to Middlesbrough for £3.45m

May, promotion to the Premier League with Middlesbrough
Middlesbrough 1997/98 season: 8 appearances, 0 goals
May 29th, final game for England v Belgium
May 31st, omitted from England World Cup 1998 squad
England 1988-1998: 57 appearances, 10 goals
August, divorce from Sheryl Gascoigne
October, admitted to Priory Hospital

1999

Middlesbrough 1998/99 season: 29 appearances, 3 goals

2000

Middlesbrough 1999/2000 season: 11 appearances, 1 goal
July, transfer to Everton (free)

2001

Everton 2000/01 season: 15 appearances, 0 goals
June, admitted to rehabilitation clinic in Cottonwood, Arizona

2002

March, transfer to Burnley (free)
Everton 2001/02 season: 23 appearances, 1 goal
Burnley 2001/02 season: 6 appearances, 0 goals

2003

March, transfer to Gansu Tianma (free)
Gansu Tianma 2002/03 season: 4 appearances, 2 goals

2004

March, player-coach at Boston United (no contract)
Boston United 2004/05 season: 5 appearances, 0 goals

2005

October–December, manager of Kettering Town

2008

February/June, sectioned under Mental Health Act

2010

July 9th, Raoul Moat incident in Rothbury, Northumberland

2014

October, sectioned under Mental Health Act

2015

May 21st, wins damages from Mirror Group over phone hacking

2019

October 17th, cleared of sexual assault charge at Teesside Crown Court

2021

December 8th, settlement reached with News Group over phone hacking

NUMBER EIGHT

DAVID BECKHAM, KENNY DALGLISH AND Cristiano Ronaldo loved number seven, while Diego Maradona, Pelé and Michel Platini loved number ten, but me? I was obsessed with number eight.

When I joined Lazio in 1992, manager Dino Zoff told me: "I'm going to give you number ten."

"No way," I replied. "I want eight."

Zoff pressed: "Number ten is a great honour in Italy. It's the number of Maradona and Pelé. Wear it with pride."

I felt like I had no choice but to relent.

"Fuck it," I thought, but within two weeks I'd broken my fibula and tibia. Call me superstitious, or plain bonkers, but I blamed that injury on the number ten.

I don't really quite know why I loved eight so much, but it was probably because other numbers carried such weight.

Along with the players I mentioned before, the number

seven is associated with Kevin Keegan, George Best and Eric Cantona, while all manner of football greats have worn number ten – Eusebio, Ferenc Puskas, and Zico to name but a few.

But number eight? No-one apart from yours truly has ever made that number their own.

I wore it nearly all the way through my career; at Newcastle United, Tottenham Hotspur, Rangers, Middlesbrough and England.

I loved looking for the number eight in the dressing room. "Ah, yes, that's my peg," I'd think to myself, when I found it.

So, when I realised there are eight primary emotions – sadness, joy, fear, disgust, anger, surprise, trust and anticipation – I thought the number would make an excellent title for this book.

Psychologist Robert Plutchick devised the concept in 1980, the year I was scouted by Newcastle United, feeling a heady mixture of what must have been both fear and joy.

The eight emotions listed by the boffin are opposites of each other – surprise v. anticipation, anger v. fear, disgust v. trust and joy v. sadness – one side versus another, a bit like football matches.

The idea is they form our core feelings, while other emotions are more or less intense versions of the primary eight.

I can't think of a better way to tell you the story of my life and I hope you enjoy reading it as much as I enjoyed writing it.

AUTHOR'S NOTE

LET'S BE HONEST, I'M KNOWN FOR MY PROWESS on the pitch, not my ability to wax lyrical on the page, so some people might be shocked to learn I love poetry. In fact, I like to think I'm a half decent poet. Gazza the poet – I know it sounds mad, but I've been in rehab more times than I care to remember. Rehab is all about reflection and I have often been encouraged to write down my thoughts in order to process them. I've written poems about all sorts, but mainly what's going on in my head. My brain is constantly whirling, it never slows, and it helps to write about stuff and try to make sense of it all. And there's a hell of a lot to make sense of.

I knew I would find it therapeutic and cathartic to write this book as I'm at a point in my life where I have nothing to hide and so much has already been said. Let's face it, I haven't always been painted in a flattering light. I've been branded a wife beater, a drug addict, an alcoholic, the list goes on. I don't think there's anything I could possibly write that could make me look much worse than I already have on many occasions.

People pay a fortune to speak to a therapist, to talk about

their problems, week after week after week. So, do you know what, why not just get everything out? How I have been feeling, what I have put myself through, what I have put others through. I may as well let people know how tough it has been at points in my life, and it might help me figure a few things out.

There's no two ways about it, I have put myself through hell. No one else has done that, I have done it to myself. I've been self-destructive, but I've also been treated badly at times – by the press, by friends who've broken my trust. I want everyone to know how I've coped with it all. If I look back at my life, fucking hell, I've gone through a lot of crazy shit, some of it bad, but a lot of it good, really good.

I have been recognised as one of the greatest players of my generation, and I will never stop being proud of that fact. From my performance in the 1990 World Cup and the decade I played for England, winning 57 caps for my country, to the joy of helping Tottenham Hotspur lift the FA Cup in 1991, and scoring a hat-trick to clinch the Scottish Premier Division for Rangers in 1996, no-one will ever take those moments away from me.

These days, I enjoy a much quieter life. I typically work a few days a month, and I spend the rest of the time doing what I love. That involves being with my manager and friend Katie and her kids, who are like family to me, just going to a soft play, or out for a meal. I also love being outdoors, going fishing and cycling when I am in good enough shape. That's when I am at my calmest, and I feel able to reflect on what has been a pretty tumultuous life, both on and off the pitch. So far, anyway. I'm only 58, so I hope I still have a while to go yet.

For the first time, I feel ready to tell you all about the sort of life I've had, so people get to know the real me, not the Gazza in the papers. Maybe I have a new career ahead of me, one as a poet or author. I know it sounds mad, but why not? It wouldn't be the craziest thing I have ever done, not by a long way.

Paul Gascoigne,
September 2025

FOREWORD

BY ALAN SHEARER

GAZZA DIDN'T JUST PLAY FOOTBALL – HE LIVED it, felt it, and breathed it in a way few ever have. He had that rare ability to make you laugh one minute, cry the next, and be completely in awe of him throughout. On the pitch, he could turn a game on its head with a single touch. Off it, he could light up a room just by walking in – sometimes for better, sometimes for worse – but always with heart.

But what people didn't always see – beneath the headlines, the humour, and the chaos – was someone with deep kindness and vulnerability. Paul has faced challenges that would have broken most, yet he's still here, still standing, and still loved by fans who remember the genius he brought to the game.

This book tells Paul's story – raw, honest, and unfiltered. It's a reminder of the joy he gave us, the pain he endured, and the legend he became.

For me, and for so many others, it's a privilege to call him a friend.

1 TRUST

PROLOGUE

TRUST – A firm belief in the reliability, truth or ability of someone or something.

DRIBBLING A BATTERED LEATHER FOOTBALL among the terraced streets of Saltwell, Gateshead, if someone had asked me about trust, I think I would have replied: "You what?"

When I was a lad, I mustn't have known the meaning of the word, and that's because I didn't need to. My younger brother Carl would go mental if I stole food from his plate for a laugh, and give me a whack, while I was always scrapping with my sisters, Lindsay and Anna. My mam, Carol, threw a vinegar bottle at the back of my head once, because I'd tried to nick some chocolate – and that's not the worst thing she's ever done to me.

But the truth is, we loved each other. It was a tough upbringing, but trust didn't even enter into it, as it was the most natural thing in the world to know my mam would look after me, no matter what, take me to Redheugh Boys' Club, and watch me play football after school. And it was a certainty my dad, John, would go out and graft, day in and day out, to put food on the table. They both grafted, to be fair, my mam more so than my dad, working four jobs at one point, just to make sure we were fed and clothed.

Playing football, I trusted every single teammate – you have to, or you'll never make it. Of course, we'd get pissed off with each other from time to time, and we'd take the mick, but that was normal, everyday banter. I never even fell out with any of the players I was up against. "You're a fat bastard," Vinnie Jones spat at me in the tunnel before he famously grabbed my balls during the Wimbledon v Newcastle game in 1988, but even that was good-hearted banter when it came down to it – nothing to be taken too seriously.

But over the years, my trust has been totally destroyed – chipped away at until I had none left, and I became a broken man, a shadow of my former self. I had trust in a lot of people until my phone started getting hacked and my friends began selling stories. That led me down a dark path, to a place where I trusted no-one, not even myself or my closest family members, and my only friends were drink and drugs. Even my ex-wife Sheryl wrote a book about me – that really fucks with your head.

Paul Merson, who I played with at Middlesborough, once said: "You do something bad to Gazza and that's it. He'll never give you another chance." And he's right, I am like that. If someone fucks about with me, that's it. I will never speak to them again.

I still remember one particular Christmas, spent alone in a hotel room, putting down my bags and walking over to the lamp on the bedside table, slowly unscrewing the bulb and peering into the socket. Next came the fire alarm, prising off the lid, convinced of what I would find in there – the bug, the recording device I just knew was listening to my every word and movement. Of course, there was nothing, but despite that, I was certain there would be and it became a ritual I repeated many times over the years.

Ironically, hotel rooms were the only place I felt safe. There were cleaners to take care of any mess that might set off my OCD, and no-one knew where to find me, but I wouldn't even order room service. I was, essentially, a prisoner in my suite, simply because I could not bring myself to trust. I had six mobile phones but would still nip out, under the cover of darkness, desperate not to be spotted, to use a public phone box. Something as simple as ordering food or a drink in a restaurant became a nightmare as I worried someone might spike my drink or put poison on my pizza. To say I became paranoid is an understatement. I thought everyone was out to get me.

I remember walking round the Metrocentre, a shopping complex in Gateshead, with my dad once, and feeling the eyes of every person in there fixed upon me, whispers behind hands, menacing expressions on faces. "Why is everyone staring at me?" I asked him, getting more and more agitated – what did these people want, were they spying on me? But my dad just said: "They're looking at you because you're Paul fucking Gascoigne, son." He was right, but I couldn't see it at the time.

I was convinced there was something sinister going on in that shopping centre.

Even now, if someone is nice or friendly towards me, I can't help but think: "What do they want?"

When I first made it big, at about two years old, (I am joking, but I was very young, still just a teenager), some people couldn't get enough of me. Then, when I fell on hard times, they would disappear, I'd never hear from them again. Since then, I've struggled to believe anyone might like me for who I actually am, rather than what they might be able to get from my wallet or the papers.

Those everyday acts of trust most people take for granted are a minefield for me. For example, I don't trust myself with a driving licence, in case I get back on the booze and decide it's a good idea to take a car or motorbike on the road. That would be a car crash, quite literally. Just the other day, I called a taxi to take me all the way up to Newcastle from Poole, a journey of 350 miles. You should have seen the look on the driver's face. Not a bad pay day for him, though, at £900. The problem is, on the train, I get pestered to death. "Gazza, Gazza, can I have a selfie?" every five minutes, it's relentless. My dad would always tell me: "Never forget where you came from, son." And that's why I can never turn one down, even when the timing is terrible, and I just want to be left alone.

And I still delete every phone message and call I get, straight away. I never answer the phone to a number I don't know – it could be the King of England, and he wouldn't be able to get through. The thing is, it sets off my OCD. It's a fucking nightmare, to be honest with you, and although I try really hard not to be nuts, I get triggered by the smallest things. I am an alcoholic, that will never change and while these days I am on the wagon more than I am off, I don't trust myself never to have another drink. All I can do is try to limit the damage when I do.

You have to trust some people, otherwise life's not worth living. The person I trust most these days is my manager and closest friend, Katie Davies. Katie and her kids have become like family to me. For the first time in my life, I don't have to worry about being screwed over. I actually encourage Katie to take more from the deals she sets up for me, when in the past with different managers I'd be fighting for a larger share of my own. She's always there for me, and she deserves it. And the people who were in my life at the very start – my mam, and my siblings, are still right there beside me. I trust them implicitly, and for that, I will always be grateful.

1

CHILDHOOD

HUDDLING ROUND THE FIRE FOR WARMTH with Carl and Anna, I stuck a piece of bread on the end of a fork and held it carefully above the flames until, slowly, it began to toast. That's how we cooked breakfast in the council house we shared in Teams, Gateshead, before my youngest sister Lindsay was born and we moved to nearby Saltwell. My great-grandad Bob Gascoigne became a nightwatchman at Sowerby Glassworks after he retired from his job as a glass blower. Him, my dad and my grandad Fred would pick up the coal which fell from the wagons and bring it home. That was lucky, as otherwise we would have been shivering our arses off during those bitter winters the North East is so famous for. They'd bring us sacks of coal, which fuelled the fire, kept us warm, cooked our food and heated our water.

We had hardly any money growing up – no TV, no microwave, no nothing, when I was really little. "Got any washing, son?" my mam would ask, and she'd throw my clothes into the bath, but only after us kids had washed in it, one after the other. She'd fill a big pan with water, and heat it over the fire, before pouring it into the bath. Each of us siblings would climb in, and get clean, then she'd start scrubbing our clothes. Every night, me, Carl and Anna would burrow under the same duvet, pushing and shoving for extra space. Fuck me, looking back, it was Victorian, but growing up like that you form really strong bonds, and that's how all these years later, my brother, my sisters, and my mam are still the closest people in my life, the ones I trust the most. My dad died of cancer in 2018 and I miss him every single day. I still become emotional every time he crosses my mind.

Things were so bad, I remember going to bingo with my mam and sitting on those uncomfortable chairs, with all the old biddies, willing our numbers to be called. "We'll have that tin of beans," my mam would say when we went to collect our prize, as food never went to waste in our house.

"You're a tramp, you are!" the other kids would yell as they waited at the gates for me after school, wanting to fight. We never had much, and I guess it must have shown in the way we dressed, the things we didn't have, but I never took it too personally. Anyway, I've come a long way since then, made millions, become an icon, scored goals which are etched into the collective memory of football fans around the world – so who's had the last laugh, eh? Not them, that's for sure.

But when I was a lad, we had nothing and so my mam, bless her, worked four jobs to keep us going. Her first was valeting cars, but she also worked in a factory making jeans, and she cleaned offices. The best job of all was the one she had in a fish and chip shop. The smell of the greasy batter was overwhelming as I entered that shop and said to my mam: "Fish and chips, please." No one knew I was her son there and she'd look at me as if she didn't know who I was and say: "That will be 15p, lad." I'd hand her the exact amount of money, and she'd give me change for £1, before scoffing the lot. Later that night, I'd be tucked up in bed, all cosy and warm, and she'd shake me awake. "Give us that money, son," she'd say. She was hard, my mam, but she would have done anything for us kids, and we loved her to bits.

I had loads of jobs myself before I signed for Newcastle United, but the one I liked the most was cleaning ice cream vans. Standing in the squeaky clean van after I'd scrubbed it until it shone, with ice cream pouring down my chin, was my favourite part. I would make myself a 99 with a chocolate flake and raspberry sauce, the works, after every shift. Actually, I'd make myself more than one, but who's keeping count. I also had a paper round before school, and I'd collect glass bottles like they were going out of fashion, because back then you could exchange them for a few pence in the shops.

The scariest job I had was doing meals on wheels when I was about nine, for 50p a day. I'd be driven round in a little van, and it was my job to knock on the doors and deliver the hot food to elderly people who couldn't get out of bed. "Come in, little son, I'll give you a sweet," they'd say, as I stood there, a tiny lad, just wanting to get back to the van. "No, thanks!" I'd tell them and scarper as quickly as I could. There were a couple of them that only had one eye, bless them, but as a kid, it terrified me. How I did that aged nine I'll never know, but I've always liked helping people. I still do now, it makes me happy.

Those jobs, along with the ones my mam had, instilled within me a strong work ethic, which has stayed with me my whole life. And if it wasn't for my parents, I don't think I would have made it as a footballer. I wouldn't have had the stomach for the hard graft.

My mam was a tough woman, fiercely protective of all of us. I remember at school once, I got into a fight with another lad, and the teacher gave us the belt six times. I came home and she went off. "How dare that teacher hit you!" she said. "I'm not pestering your dad with this, he's in the pub having a drink." So instead she decided to go and find that headteacher herself. Nobody was going to hit her son and get away with it! We went and found the headteacher, God knows how. He was a rugby player and all but that didn't give my mam even a moment's pause. "You hit my son, did you?" she said and then she had a right go at him and told him to fuck off. I can't even imagine what that teacher thought at the time but it felt good knowing she was on my side, no matter what.

She really was an unbelievable mother, the best in the world, but we had our fair share of fights. She might not have tolerated anyone else hitting me, but that didn't stop her from raising her hand to me herself. I tell her now: "Mam, you were like John Wayne with a slipper, you never fucking missed." When she tried to whack me, I would put my arm up as a reflex to protect myself. "Put your arm down when I hit you!" she'd yell. Yes, she could be a hard woman, my mam.

But she loved me so much – she still does – and I've never doubted that fact, not for a second. I remember her standing at the sidelines, drenched to the bone at times, as she watched me play football, determined to stay until the end of the game. One day she came home clutching a red, white and blue box containing my first ever pair of football boots. Opening up the cardboard box, the excitement welled inside me as I realised it held a pair of shiny leather Patrick boots. "Mam, you're a diamond!" I told her, giving her a big hug. They weren't cheap and she must have worked like a mad woman to get the money to buy them. Kevin Keegan, my hero, was sponsored by Patrick at that time and they were my favourite brand. Every day, without fail, I'd pick up some polish and a brush, and clean those boots until I could see my face in them.

I fought like cat and dog with my sister Anna and I was obsessed with *Match of the Day*. Me and Anna would have mad rows about it, she'd always want to watch something different, but we had a laugh together too. We'd put shows on in our back garden for our elderly neighbours – though looking back, I'm not sure what they must have thought of it all. They'd pay 2p each to watch us carry on and I was always the star, as making people laugh was the thing I liked to do the most. I'd take all my clothes off, appear at the door and say: "Hello, girls!" then I'd run away. I was only about eight.

We'd also go carol singing pretty much all year round, just to get a bit of extra money. It would be the height of summer and we'd be knocking on people's doors singing, 'We Wish you a Merry Christmas'. The neighbours would say: "You do know it's June?" But we'd do anything for a bit of extra cash back then, as things were really tight. Anna was into gymnastics when we were kids, that's all she did, and Lindsay, my little sister, was the spoiled one, our mam's pet. She was six years younger, while there's only a year or so between me and Anna. I'd get jealous and take it out on Lindsay, because she had all the attention. Carl, my brother, tended to do his own thing. When we were really young we'd play football together, just me and him in the streets, kicking a ball around. Then he got into his own crowd at school, and I didn't see as much of him. He's driven me mad at times as well, but I love him just as much as my sisters.

I remember once my mam bought us each a goldfish. We took them out of the bowl, put them on the table, and we said, right, whichever fish gets the furthest, the owner wins a bag of crisps. I don't think those poor fish survived, but that's the kind of crazy stuff we'd get up to.

Another time, when Carl was about 12, my mouth was watering like mad as mam put egg and chips for us on the table. It was one of my favourite meals, and I ate mine quickly, never taking my eye off my brother. Then, I saw he had a single chip left on his plate. It called to me, that chip, slathered in salt and vinegar, begging to be eaten. So I leant over and I just fucking grabbed it, I couldn't help myself. "You bastard!" yelled Carl and threw a fork at my head. I tried to get it out but it was stuck fast. "Mam," I shouted. "There's a fork stuck in my head!" She came and yanked it out, and I got another bollocking. I've got loads of scars on my forehead, mainly from drunken accidents over the years, but that was one of the first.

I was in hospital a lot as a kid. I've had six broken arms, and I was always going to the Queen Elizabeth Hospital in Gateshead with one injury or another. I got my first broken arm aged five when I was playing on apparatus in the gym and climbed up high, only to fall down. The second time I broke my arm it was in Saltwell Park, close to where we lived back then. "Mam, I am going to the park," I called as I left the house. "Behave yourself," she said but as usual, I didn't listen. Me and my friends were playing a game to see if we could swing from one tree to another. I thought, I can do that, easy. I swung from one branch and tried to grab the next, but I hadn't realised my legs had gone up really high, and I just fell to the ground. I ran all the way home with a broken arm. I was always doing daft things and getting injured, but I just got on with it. My mam would say: "Son, are you going to be alreet?"

"Yeah, I will be alreet," I'd tell her. I never complained and it stood me in good stead for what the future had in store.

I was a mischief-maker when I was a lad, I'd get something in my head and I'd just have to do it.

I went to Heathfield Senior High School, and I never really got bullied, but there was this one kid who was convinced he was a hard bastard. I was about 13, I don't like saying that number because of my OCD, but that's the age I was when we were doing metal work and this guy was just goading me. "I'm a hard bastard," he kept saying, over and over. Something inside me snapped, and I took a piece of metal, and put it down my jumper. He punched me, but to his horror his fist hit the metal, not my stomach. He broke his arm and I got suspended for a week, but it wasn't the first time, and it wouldn't be the last.

At school I was mostly a prankster, laughing and joking, but I was really good at sport, not just football. I got loads of trophies for tennis, badminton, table tennis. I was captain of the school football team, and I scored goals for fun. It was the same at primary school. At the age of eight, I'd score about 15 goals per game. It was too easy. My mam would always be watching on the touchline, and she'd take me home afterwards.

My dad was a hod carrier and one of the hardest men in the North East. Everyone knew who he was in those days. I didn't see much of him, as he was always working or in the pub. It was my mam who came to all the football games. My dad didn't watch as often because he didn't like crowds of people. He was a hard bastard, dry as anything, but I miss him so much, even now. He was a proper grafter, my dad, but things changed once he fell ill, and he struggled to work after that.

It was lucky, the day he took a bad turn, that I was off school. He was having a seizure and my mam said: "Quick, Paul, put your fingers in his mouth to stop him swallowing his tongue." I did it – I've still got the fucking bite marks. He wouldn't let go of me, he was like a Rottweiler.

"Mam," I said. "I can't get my fingers out of his mouth." His jaw had just locked up, but eventually, my mam was able to force it open. He was in hospital for six months, which was a tough time for all the family. It was a struggle for the doctors to work out what was wrong with him, and he was never the same again after that.

When I started earning enough money I paid for my dad to go private and they found a big clump of varicose veins in his head, which was causing him to haemorrhage. They also came across three aneurysms, and we were told it was a miracle he survived. He had major surgery to seal them up, and to remove the varicose veins. "Most people don't survive one aneurysm, let alone three," the doctor told us. Just like me, my dad was a man who had nine lives.

He did get better, my dad, but he never fully recovered. He and my mam were always splitting up and getting back together again. They'd have huge rows and for a while Dad went to live in the Crown Pub in Gateshead with another woman. He did come back after that but eventually he left for good. After his big operation, I reckon he thought, "fuck it, I don't want to get involved in any more arguments," and he was off.

I eventually bought Carl, Anna, Mam and Dad houses really close to each other in Dunston, and aside from my dad, they're all still living there now. Lindsay lives nearby as well but I didn't have to buy her a property as she already had one.

It was funny, you'd think they would have hated living so close to each other after they split up, but my mam and dad loved being neighbours – they stopped being a married couple and became best friends.

I remember saying to my parents, aged just 14: "When I become the best player in the world, you two will never work again." I don't know if they believed me or not, but by the time I was 17, I'd been proven right.

That's one of the things I'm most proud of, being able to help out my family. They are the only people in my life, apart from my agent Katie, that I've been able to trust. That trust was rocked big time when my phone got hacked, and I accused them of selling stories about me. But even though I've put them through absolute hell over the years, with the drinking, cocaine, and other daft antics, they've always stood by me. They're still standing by me now, thank God.

2

EARLY CAREER

"WHAT ON EARTH ARE YOU DOING, GASCOIGNE?" my teacher Mr Hepworth yelled as I sat with my head bowed, writing my signature over and over in his geography lesson.

"I'm practising my autograph," I told him. "I'm going to be a professional football player."

"No, you're not, lad," he replied. "Only one in a million make it as a professional football player."

"Yeah," I said. "And I am going to be that one."

Aside from my family, something else I've always been able to trust in is my talent as a footballer. I was a cocky bastard and I never doubted it for a second, even as a kid. I was 14 then, and I already knew I was going to make it big, really big. And as my career took off, I never forgot what that teacher said to me.

Fast forward ten years and I am standing in Dunston Park, all alone, as the light begins to fade, tears in my eyes. It's 1990 and I have just returned to Gateshead from the World Cup a hero and a household name. It's good to be back and see my family, but I need a moment alone, to reflect. I look around the park, the paths I'd dribble a football along as a lad, the silhouette of St James' Park in the background, and think: "This is where it all began." It is a place so familiar to me after the excitement of Italy, I am overcome by emotion, and I remember the words my dad said to me, as I was on the cusp of stardom: "Never forget where you came from, son." This is where I came from, I think to myself, as darkness falls, and I'm proud of it too.

At some point, while I was back home, I got it in my head to return to Heathfield Senior High School to confront Mr Hepworth. Not knowing if he was even still teaching there, I walked straight through the old school gates, with the kids going wild, cheering and asking for my autograph. I found the classroom where I'd sat bored as anything in his Geography lessons all those years ago, and peered through the window. I couldn't believe it – there he was, the old bastard, standing in front of the blackboard, as though time had stood still.

I knocked on the glass, opened the door and said: "Do you remember me, you bastard? Do you remember what you said to me?"

"Yes, I remember," he sighed.

"Please never say that to another pupil ever again," I told him, to the laughter and delight of all the kids in that room. I went back every day after that for about a week, and as I was one of the most famous people in the country, the whole school erupted each time.

"Please stop coming here," Mr Hepworth would beg. I tortured that man but he deserved it, to be fair, after what he said to me.

Despite my rise to global fame, it felt like just yesterday I'd been playing football with a tennis ball, spending hours kicking it against a wall, or dribbling it through the back lanes of Saltwell. It was tricky trying to play football with such a tiny ball, but I'd be at it all evening, even after it fell dark, and it barely left my foot. I'd be eating my tea and playing with that ball under the kitchen table. Then, when I was seven, my dad went to Germany to work, just like in *Auf Wiedersehen, Pet* – that comedy with Tim Healy and Jimmy Nail. When he came home, he gave me the best present anyone has ever given me – a leather football.

I loved that football to death, and took it with me everywhere I went. After playing with the tennis ball, the football was easy peasy, so much better to handle, and I became completely obsessed.

"Time for bed, son," my mam would say, as I climbed the stairs. "Night, Mam," I'd call, as I entered my room, only to open the window, throw my football onto the grass below, and reach for the drainpipe. I'd shimmy down, and be out for hours, playing in the streets until I could barely stand. Then, I'd climb back up the drainpipe and finally go to sleep. Either that, or Lindsay and I would leap out of the window and land on a mattress we'd put in the garden, escaping into the night that way. Lindsay loved to watch me play, and kick a ball about herself, and it was good to have company at times.

When I got the football off my dad, I kept it to myself, I wouldn't let anyone touch it and I dribbled it wherever I went. I'd run to school with it, kick it back and forth along walls, all the way there, and then hide it, so the teacher didn't see it and take it from me. Then, I'd do it all over again on the way home.

I will always remember playing in the streets, a young lad, on my own, to the almighty roar of the crowd from St James' Park, just over the river, and being transported on to the pitch. As I belted the ball into the back of an imaginary net, the fans were going wild for me, not Malcolm Macdonald, Alan Gowling or whoever it was who'd actually scored at the football stadium. I was just a schoolboy, but in my head, I was already the hero, the star of the match.

When I watched Holland's Johan Cruyff perform his famous 'Cruyff turn' on the telly, leaving a Swedish defender bamboozled during the 1974 World Cup, I was desperate to master the technique myself, and I did, just kicking a ball around outside. Years later, in the 1990 World Cup, I did the exact same trick – against the Dutch, no less – and it helped turn me into a superstar. "Who is this lad?" they all thought. Well, I got the same reaction when I did it as a kid, too.

Where I lived, in Dunston, was still a canny way from St James' Park, which was on the other side of the River Tyne, but in those days the explosion of sound from the Gallowgate End was fucking unbelievable, the noise it made.

Newcastle United had an exciting side when I was a lad, featuring top players such as Supermac and Bobby Moncur, and were managed by the legendary Joe Harvey, who had twice led us to FA Cup glory as a player in the 1950s. As manager, he also won the Fairs Cup for the Magpies in 1969 – the last trophy the club was to clinch for over 50 years.

The club had made it to the 1974 FA Cup final, where they were trounced 3-0 by Bill Shankly's Liverpool. They also reached the final of the League Cup in 1976, but within two years, Newcastle had been relegated to Division Two, lost all their star players, and then spent the rest of the decade in the doldrums.

Aged nine, I was desperate to get into Redheugh Boys' Club, rivals to the famous Wallsend Boys' Club which has produced the likes of Alan Shearer, Peter Beardsley and Steve Bruce, but I was two years too young. I'd climb over the wall to watch them train, longing to be involved.

"Mam, Dad, you have to get me into that team," I begged. Eventually, my dad took me along.

"This lad's 11," he told the coach. "I know he looks a bit young, but he's a late developer, small for his age."

To begin with, I just acted as a ball boy, doing odd jobs, such as putting up the nets, but eventually I got into the club. It was brilliant playing for an actual team, alongside other players, on a proper pitch, rather than with my mates in the park, or on my own in the street.

My mam or dad would take me every single night, handing over 2p each time. I was a chubby little kid, but I was powerful on the pitch, and I stood out, even though some of the other players would take the piss. "Corned beef legs!" they'd yell, as my limbs turned purple and blue in the cold, but that didn't stop me scoring goals and getting myself noticed.

At the age of 12, I tried to remember to breathe as a crowd of around 365 watched me take a penalty for Redheugh Boys'. Willing myself to stay calm, I gave the ball an almighty whack, and to my relief and pride, it flew through the air, hitting the back of the net to ecstatic cheers from the sidelines. As a result, I won my first ever trophy, which was presented to me by Chris Waddle, who played for Tow Law Town, in Bishop Auckland at that time. As fate would have it, I ended up rooming with him during the 1990 World Cup. "Remember when you gave us that trophy, Chris?" I'd say. "Aye," he'd reply. I've still got that trophy, it's one of the most precious things I own.

Football scouts were regular visitors to Redheugh Boys' as well as Gateshead Boys', where I also played. I did trials for Ipswich, Middlesbrough and Southampton early on, but none of them came to anything.

In 1980, I was finally spotted by Newcastle United. There was a knock at the door and to my amazement it was a scout from the club. But my dad just looked at him and said: "What took you so long?" I started training with the club every week after school, and I eventually got the chance to be a ball boy during a home game. Throwing the ball back to my heroes, while the crowd roared in my ears, not in the distance from the streets of Gateshead, where I lived, was electrifying. "I want a bit of this," I thought to myself. And I got it, to be fair.

Arthur Cox took over as Newcastle manager in September of that year and under his stewardship the club's fortunes finally got back on track. He oversaw the emergence of a young Chris Waddle, persuaded England captain Kevin Keegan to join us in 1982 – what a coup that was! – and also brought in quality players such as Terry McDermott, David McCreery, Glenn Roeder and Peter Beardsley. It was a club now on the rise, having spent so many years floundering.

I started having serious talks with Newcastle about joining the club as an apprentice at 16, once I left school. In the end, I signed up on my 16th birthday, with my mam and dad in the room, giving each other daggers as they were on one of their breaks, much to the bemusement of Willie McFaul, a coach at the club.

I was paid £25 a week by Newcastle United, which seemed like a fortune at the time, but as I was still living at home, they paid my mam £35 for my keep, £10 more than me!

"Mam," I'd say. "How come you're getting £35 a week, and I am only getting £25?"

"I feed you," she'd reply.

"What, fucking beans on toast?" I'd say.

"At least I feed you," she'd shoot back.

It was at that moment when life changed forever, and my family finally stopped having to worry about money. I'd already fulfilled the promise I made when I was a lad, that I'd make sure my mam and dad would never have to work again. It was fortunate, because by that point, my dad wasn't very well. I took good care of him from then on, because if it hadn't been for that leather football he bought me, I'd never have made it.

He was obsessed with cars, my dad, I think he had about 82 from me, all told. He was a twat with cars. Three times a year, I would shit a brick. Father's Day, his birthday and fucking Christmas, I didn't know what bill was coming through the post. I think his last car was £75k or something, a BMW. I got a shock when that bill landed.

"It's my Father's Day present," he told me.

I went: "Oh, God," but I didn't mind, really, I just wanted to help him out, he'd done so much for me.

Once I joined Newcastle United, I made a name for myself in the youth team, and I was chosen to be captain during our 1984/85 FA Youth Cup run. I scored twice against Watford in the final at Vicarage Road, and we won that game 4-1. It was the last time Newcastle United lifted the FA Youth Cup – no team has done it since.

Afterwards, I remember sitting in the bath with the trophy, and Elton John came into the dressing room. He was the chairman of Watford at that time, and he wanted to congratulate the team. I was naked in the bath when he poked his head in and said: "Well done, son."

I was made up to see him, and I said: "Give us a song, Elton. Come on, give us a song."

But he got all embarrassed and shot off.

"Come back!" I shouted, but he was gone.

I heard from him again after the World Cup in 1990, when he called me up and said: "Paul, if you want to come and stay with me and my boyfriend, you're very welcome."

Fuck that, I thought – Elton's a good lad, but I didn't fancy it!

After the Watford game, the Newcastle manager Jack Charlton said: "Come with me, you're playing against Norwich tomorrow, for the first team."

I panicked a bit and said: "Ah, no, I want to go back with the youth team and celebrate."

I suppose I did doubt myself at times, but I knew straight away I was going to be good. I'd do anything to win, put the other guys off. I used to take the piss out of the players all the time and I would talk non-stop as I was playing football. "I'm going out with your girlfriend," I'd tell them, as they tried to tackle me. "I'm having sex with your girlfriend," I'd say, over and over.

"No, you're not!" they'd yell back, but it would distract them from their game. They'd put their head down and I would be away with the ball – I played like that all the way through, right to the end.

I worked like a bastard, as well, training hard at night. When

I first joined the youth team Jack Charlton said to me: "I heard you are a good player."

"Yeah, I am," I replied.

"How long have you got left on your contract?" he asked.

"Two years," I told him.

"No, you've not, you fat bastard," he said. "You've got two weeks. Start losing weight."

I was chubby back then, for a football player. I loved Mars bars and my chippy teas too much. At that time, my regular diet was a packet of Minstrels, fish and chips, and a bottle of cola.

Jack Charlton made me train with Brendan Foster, the long distance runner who founded the Great North Run. He'd come to the house at 6pm three times a week, and we would run six miles to the running track. Once there, I'd do 30 laps – he'd train me so hard. Then I'd go home and train at 11pm with a bin bag on, to try and sweat some of the weight off. It was tough, but it was worth it. Within months, I was captain of the youth team, captain of the reserve team, and was ready to play for the first team.

My contract was renewed and I started playing regularly for the first team in 1985/86. As I got more and more experience, I began winning Man of the Match awards, against the big teams too – Liverpool, Tottenham and Manchester United. That helped me believe in myself, but I always did anyway. I had a hell of a lot of trust I was going to make it big in the early days and I was proved right. No matter what happened to me in my life I never lost that early trust I had in my talent, and to this day, I still believe there was no-one better than me at football – I was the best in the world.

3
—

TRUST DESTROYED

WEARING A DAFT GREEN ELF SUIT, I CHUCKLED
away to myself as I drove to my dad's house one Christmas,
wanting to surprise my little nephews. I'd rung him up on my
way there and said: "I'll be with you about 2pm, don't tell the
bairns. I want to see the looks on their faces when they see me
dressed as a mad bastard."

I was looking forward to spending the whole of Christmas
with my family in Dunston, on the street where they all had
houses, and excited for a big Gascoigne get-together. But as I
got closer to my dad's, I could see something was wrong, terribly
wrong, and a wave of nausea washed over me.

There was a group of people standing outside the house,
looking expectant, like they were waiting for someone to arrive.
"It can't be, it can't be," I thought to myself, but as I got closer,
the truth hit me like a smack in the mouth.

There was a pack of photographers standing around on the

street, cameras slung over their shoulders, stamping their feet in the cold.

"What the fuck?" I thought to myself. The only person I'd told where I was going, looking like a silly bugger in a Santa's elf costume, was my dad. How had the press found out? I turned the car round and rang him straight away, though the photographers had spotted me by this point and were following me now, the twats. "How the fuck did the press know I was coming to your house?" I demanded. He'd opened the curtains by then, and seen them all, hanging about, on the pavement. "I don't fucking know!" he replied. "I haven't told them, I haven't told anyone," he insisted. "But no-one else knew, other than you. You're the only person I rang," I said, starting to panic. Could it really be the case that my family, the people I trusted above all others, were tipping off the press about me?

"Dad," I said. "I don't know what's going on, but I don't trust you. I don't trust any of you. I can't spend Christmas with you feeling like this. I'd rather be on my own, in a hotel."

"Son," he pleaded. "Don't be daft. We would never, ever do that to you. Come back, please."

Tears streaming down my face, I drove to the Travelodge on Newcastle's Quayside, and got myself a room, still dressed like an elf. The receptionist must have thought I was the saddest bastard that ever lived. By this point, I had already become a paranoid nutcase, suspecting the press had me bugged, and hotels had become my refuge. As I said before, I like how everything is neat and clean in a hotel because I need places to be spotless all the time. Mess and dirt sets off my OCD, so I love the fact hotel rooms are cleaned every day. There's also an anonymity about them, an ease, and having travelled all over the world for football, they're familiar to me and in a way, they feel like a home from home.

That said, the Christmas I spent alone in a Travelodge room, with my family just over the river, in Gateshead, celebrating without me, was one of the most miserable of my entire life. Gascoigne Christmases were always magical, and my favourite part was lavishing everyone with presents, the more extravagant the better. I just loved to see them happy, but that Christmas no fucker had a smile on their face – not me, and certainly not my family, not after what I had accused them of.

It wasn't the first time, and it wouldn't be the last, that I suspected my family of screwing me over, which I now know was heartbreaking for them all. But it drove me mad that the press seemed to be aware of my every movement, and there was no logical explanation for it. Whenever I mentioned to someone where I was going, what I was doing – bang, photographers would be there.

"Right Dad, I'm going fishing in Rothbury," I'd tell him.

I'd head off, but when I arrived, the press would already be waiting for me, by a river in the middle of fucking nowhere.

"What the fuck is going on?" I'd think to myself. I didn't want to suspect my dad, but he was the only person I'd mentioned it to.

Another time, I told him: "I am going to Hawaii for a holiday, I'll let you know where I am in case you need me." I gave him the details of the hotel, not thinking much of it.

But after I checked in, it became obvious the person in the room next door to mine was a journalist, there to spy on me. Another time I got talking to a girl, just one lass, and we arranged to meet up in London. I turned up to find three photographers there, taking pictures – I'm not doing that again, I thought.

38

But most of all, I blamed my mam and dad, and my closest friends. I'd be talking to them about something specific, daft even, and then a few days later it would end up in the papers. "You're the only ones I've spoken to," I'd tell them. "How is this happening!"

"Come on, son," my mam would say. "You must know it's not us. You're not thinking straight."

The accusations caused fierce arguments between my mam and dad and siblings. I blamed all of them, but unbeknown to me at the time, they were also blaming each other. It was heartbreaking as the Gascoignes had always stood together no matter what – now this was tearing us apart.

My mam was in a bad way, and she even stopped leaving the house as she suspected her friends were feeding information to the press. Her relationship with my dad was already under strain because of the brain surgery he'd had, and the massive toll that had taken on his physical and mental health. I'll never know for sure, but I believe the stories in the papers and the arguments they caused were the final nails in the coffin when it came to the breakdown of their marriage.

It had got to the point where I didn't trust any of them, not my friends, and not my family. I didn't want to speak to anyone, not even my best mate Jimmy Five Bellies Gardner, or my kids – the paranoia I felt was overwhelming. I'd also come to realise there was something more sinister going on than those closest to me leaking stories to the press, though that was bad enough. By this point I had become convinced I was under surveillance. I was positive journalists were somehow able to listen into my phone calls, and even suspected them of bugging my hotel rooms. I went to London and spent around £60k on gadgets.

I was on a mad mission to find out what was going on and I bought a hidden camera and listening devices.

But to be honest, the gadgets made my paranoia even worse, because they just fuelled my obsession, while failing to provide any concrete information. I ended up with six mobile phones, but I never knew which one was going to be compromised, so I'd still go out and use a phone box – it was embarrassing.

Even my home phone wasn't safe. I rang up British Telecom and said: "Do us a favour, will you, and change my number? I have had enough of the press, they have got hold of it." But within 15 minutes of doing that, the *News of the World* was ringing up on the new number. I just thought, the fucking bastards.

I knew the journalists would stop at nothing to get a story – even if it was just something silly, like me turning up at my dad's house dressed like an elf. But that didn't prevent me from blaming my family as well – I was hurt, scared, and lashing out at everyone around me.

Lindsay had told me something very disturbing, which had happened shortly after my wedding. She said she was at home when she got a call on her landline phone from my mate, the Liverpool player Steve McManaman.

"Hiya Lindsay," he said, in his scouse accent. "How are you doing? Did you enjoy the wedding? What a fantastic day!"

"Yeah, it was brilliant," said Lindsay.

"Listen, do you know where Paul is? Is he with you? I can't get hold of him," Steve told her.

"I've no idea," said Lindsay – at this point she was still living in Gateshead, and I was in Scotland, with Rangers. Lindsay had no clue where I was, or what I was up to.

Steve then started asking silly questions, obviously fishing for any information he could get out of her – that's when Lindsay realised something wasn't quite right.

She rang me up straight away, and told me about the strange conversation she'd had with my friend. I knew immediately Steve would never have called Lindsay to ask where I was. The thought was ridiculous, and I was convinced a sneaky bastard journalist must have been pretending to be him. I checked with Steve anyway, and sure enough, he had absolutely no idea what I was talking about.

"Just be really careful," I told Lindsay. "Don't say anything to anyone. The reporters are sly bastards. They'll do anything for a headline."

I was in such a bad way I turned to drink and drugs big time, and started spending lots of time in hotels. It sounds miserable as hell, and it was, but they were the only places I felt safe, so in a way, I didn't mind it. I'd check in, go to the room, and take the landline phone off the hook. I would nip out and quickly get some food, but I never ordered room service. I would tell the staff: "If anyone rings reception for me, say I'm not here." I tried checking in under a false name, but that was a daft idea as everyone knew exactly who I was. I would constantly change my numbers and was always spending an absolute fortune on SIM cards.

At one point, in 2008, I went on a cocaine binge for a month, travelling from hotel to hotel. For weeks, all I did was snort coke and down booze. The final straw came as I lay on a hotel bed, eating a packet of wine gums. All of a sudden, one of them, I think it was a red one, appeared to spring to life and started to talk. "How are you Paul?" said the wine gum. "Ah, shit," I thought to myself, "I really do need help."

I called my dad and ended up getting sectioned, which was probably the best thing that could have happened to me. As you can imagine, I felt quite at home in the nut house, and it sobered me up, but it didn't get rid of the root cause of my problems.

The worst thing was nobody believed me when I told them my phone was being hacked, and the loneliness I experienced was overwhelming. My own counsellor even accused me of paranoia, and blamed it on the drugs – but it was the hacking which had led me to the drugs in the first place.

People say: "Well, you didn't have to drink and do drugs." But of course I had to. What choice did I have? I couldn't go anywhere, couldn't do anything, couldn't even fucking ring anyone. All I could do was sit in the house, or a hotel room and anyone who knows me understands that's exactly what drives me crazy.

I stopped eating in restaurants in case my food got spiked. That's how bad the paranoia became – even when I was with my kids, I wouldn't eat.

I'd be sitting in a cafe with my daughter Bianca and she'd say: "Dad, what kind of sandwich do you want?"

"Don't want one, darlin'," I'd tell her.

I couldn't eat and it was hell. I used to be 12st 7lbs, but I became a scrawny bastard, barely weighing 9st and I didn't recognise myself.

I was on the phone to the police almost constantly and eventually Scotland Yard confirmed they had proof that the newspapers had been listening into my voicemails, and the feeling of vindication was overwhelming.

Then, in 2011, the phone hacking scandal made headlines

around the world. It emerged the *News of the World* had illegally listened to the private voicemails of loads of celebs, politicians, even the Royal family. Finally, people began to realise I wasn't such a mad bastard after all.

But the public finally sat up and took notice when they discovered missing schoolgirl Milly Dowler's phone had been hacked, messing with the police investigation. She was only a kid of 13 and her body was discovered six months after her death in a wood in Yateley Heath, Hampshire, in September 2002. She'd been raped and murdered by a sick fucker called Levi Bellfield. No one could stomach that, least of all me. What they did to me was bad enough, never mind a murdered lass.

Then, in 2014, a load of journalists got banged up, including Andy Coulson, the guy in charge of the *News of the World*, so I was made up about that.

Along with lots of other famous people, including Sienna Miller, Prince Harry, Sean Bean and Hugh Grant, I decided to sue the News Group Newspapers, the publisher of the *News of the World*. Gerald Shamash, my lawyer, worked on the case for me, and the High Court in London ruled in my favour. However, 15 years later I am still waiting for that payout. I am expecting to receive it around next January – better late than never.

In 2015, I also successfully sued Mirror Group News (MGN), along with seven other high profile people, including Sadie Frost and Shane Ritchie. The High Court awarded me a significant sum for stories published as a result of hacking my phone on that occasion.

I have never fully recovered from the consequences of the media intrusion and surveillance. I am still a paranoid bastard, always looking over my shoulder, never fully trusting anyone. I change my number roughly every six months to a year and I only share it with close family and friends.

Every time I send someone a text message, I delete it straight away, so there's nothing stored on my phone and when I get a text, I get rid of it immediately. It's fucking horrible to be honest with you, as it sets off my OCD and that drives me nuts.

It took me years, but I do now trust in my family and in Katie. I'm actually closer to my family now, as a result of what we went through and I am so grateful for those relationships, but I will live with the consequences of phone hacking forever. I don't think I will ever fully recover, I'm a distrustful sod now, and I reckon I will be for as long as I live.

4

AGENTS

"GO WITH MEL AND LEN," MY GOOD MATE Chris Waddle told me. "They'll really get you moving." Chris was seven years older than me, and I played with him for a short while at Newcastle United before he moved to Tottenham. I looked up to him, and took his advice seriously.

Mel Stein and Len Lazarus were Chris's agents, and he seemed happy enough with them, so as a young lad on the rise at Newcastle United, knowing I needed representation, they seemed as good a choice as any.

Mel and Len were the first of a string of agents I had over the years, and although they had some good points, and made me a shedload of money over the years, it wasn't until I started working with Katie Davies that I finally found one I could trust with my life. When you think about it, it's mad it took three decades for that to happen. Mel was a lawyer and Len was an accountant and they were as thick as thieves, those two, which is funny because normally lawyers and accountants hate each other. If I said: "Mel, I have a problem with Len," he wouldn't do a thing about it, and vice versa.

Mel and Len handled my transfer from Newcastle United to Tottenham Hotspur in July 1988, and got me a £100k signing-on fee, which I was chuffed to bits with. The transfer fee was a record £2.2million, the most a British club had ever paid for a player. My wages were around £2.5k a week, when appearance cash was taken into account, and as I'd only been getting £120 at Newcastle, it was a massive increase.

Mel and Len were with me a long time, and they also handled my transfer from Tottenham to Lazio in 1992. The Italians paid £5.5million for me, quite a lot less than the figure of £8.5million which had been agreed on before I injured my knee, delaying my debut with the club for over a year.

They also offered a signing-on fee of about £780k, which I thought was a bit crap given Lazio had saved £3million on the transfer.

At the same time, I was getting approaches from other places and there was even an offer of around £20million to join Grampus Eight in Japan. It was a good team, Gary Lineker played for them when he left Tottenham, but I didn't fancy Japan. I wanted to be closer to home, in Italy.

"Am I really only getting a £780k signing-on fee?" I asked Len. "Seems a bit rubbish, taking everything into consideration."

"That's as much as we've been able to get," he told me. "We tried our best."

I decided to go to Lazio directly as I had nothing to lose – I knew they'd had their eye on me for a while and were desperate for me to join them. I rang them up, cheeky bastard that I am, and said: "I want more money, a signing-on fee of at least £2million for starters."

Lazio agreed immediately to my demand, as well as a weekly wage of £22k. I was in a contract with Mel and Len, and so they also negotiated the fees when I moved to Rangers in 1995 and Middlesbrough in 1998. I joined Everton in 2000 on a free transfer after my contract with Middlesbrough came to an end, so they didn't make any money out of me on that occasion.

It was around the time I moved to Goodison Park that I fell out with Mel and Len and we parted ways. So I didn't have an agent for a while. I had enough money in the bank, I didn't think I needed one.

Various agents came and went, none of them for very long until, in the early 2000s, Terry and Freda Baker, a married couple who ran A1 Sporting Speakers, arrived on the scene. After my football career came to an end, Terry and Freda arranged for me to speak about my life at venues across the country.

The money was decent, and I enjoyed it, to be fair, spending time with the fans, who'd never stopped loving me, despite all my problems. Walking onto the stage amid raucous applause, a microphone in hand, my heart would thud madly in my chest. I'd be in a bad way at times, drunk and miserable, and have to drag myself out of my hotel room but it was nearly always worth it, just to hear the audience cheer and erupt in laughter at my mad tales about my footballing years.

On one occasion at a venue, I was languishing in my bed, drunk and trying to summon the courage to get myself to the stage when, all of a sudden, there was a knock at the door.

It was 2018 and I'd already decided by this point I wanted

to leave Terry and Freda as I wasn't happy – I just didn't know how or when.

"Who is it, what do you want?" I asked, as a friendly looking fella came into the room with a smile on his face.

"I'm Shane Whitfield, an agent," he told me. "I set up this venue."

"Ah, yes," I said. "I saw you selling memorabilia in the foyer. It's a decent venue, this is."

"Listen, Gazza," he replied. "I'll pay you a bit more than Terry for these events, if you sign with me."

That's when I decided to leave A1 Sporting Speakers and work with Shane instead. It seemed like the perfect opportunity at the time. However, Shane was to break my trust, and in the most shocking way.

5

TRUSTING KATIE

STAGGERING AROUND MY DISMAL FLAT IN Bournemouth I picked up the gin bottle from the kitchen counter and poured myself another glass. I was already in a bad way, but I was still awake which meant I would keep necking booze until I passed out. I took a generous gulp but instantly realised something was very wrong and spat the liquid into the sink. This wasn't gin at all, it was water!

"The bitch!" I yelled, reaching for my phone to call my friend Katie Davies.

"You poured my gin away and filled up the bottle with water. How dare you, you cow!" I spat down the phone when she answered.

"It's for your own good, Paul. You're killing yourself," she pleaded.

I hung up and started ransacking the flat in a desperate bid to find something else to drink. Ideally, something which was at least 30 per cent proof. It had become a familiar scenario. I'd be in the middle of a drinking binge, only to discover I'd run out of alcohol because Katie had taken it upon herself to get rid of it.

I was in a bad way when Katie came into my life, a really bad way. I was drinking heavily and living in a council flat after being ordered to stay in Bournemouth by a judge. I'd been caught drunk in a car in Newcastle and ended up in court. I lost my licence and was told I had to leave Newcastle and live in Bournemouth, close to the rehab facility the Providence Project, where I'd managed to get sober before.

But at this point, in 2014, I was struggling to do anything much other than drink, and I had no-one in my life. I'd turned into a sad bastard, a shadow of my former self. All that changed when I spotted Katie while getting myself a coffee on one of the days I was trying to pull myself together. I won't lie, Katie was and still is an absolutely stunning girl. I think that's probably why I was drawn to her first of all, but when we got talking it was like I had already known her for years.

I wasn't wearing any of the flash jewellery I sometimes have on and to a youngster like her – she was only 21 at the time – I must have seemed like an average guy down on his luck.

"Excuse me, mate," a man interrupted. "Can I have your autograph?"

"No problem," I replied, as Katie watched on bemused.

"Are you famous?" she asked me.

"Yeah," I replied. "I used to play football."

Katie had heard of me, but she didn't really know who I was, which helped me to trust her. She clearly wasn't after my money – I didn't have much at that point, anyway – or the kudos of spending time with me. It turned out I had dated her auntie for a while, and we exchanged numbers, agreeing to meet up again.

We saw each other regularly from then on. Katie, who was mam to a little boy, was a student and had the time to meet up during the day. We laughed and joked around with each other constantly, we were never serious. It helped take my mind off the mess my life had become. From the start, we simply hit it off as friends – there was never anything more between us, we just got on. But as our friendship deepened, Katie began to take on a more serious role in my life.

One night, drunk and engulfed by an overwhelming misery, I rang her up and said: "Katie, I don't want to do this any more. I don't want to live."

She dragged herself out of bed and drove round to my flat, cleared up the mess and put me to bed.

Katie could see I was in a dark place, struggling badly with the drink, and she helped me out a lot. I'd be sitting there, at 1am, needing a friend, and I'd ring her up. Bless her, she'd come straight round in the middle of the night to check I was OK. She visited most days, bringing me food and soft drinks and yes, she'd pour away my gin and fill the bottles up with water. I'd be raging when I realised later on, but deep down I knew she was just trying to help and that was because she cared.

"You need to get sober," Katie would say. No shit, I'd think, it isn't that easy, but Katie did whatever she could. She got me out of the house, introduced me to the guy she was married to at the time, Matt, who also became a good friend, as well as her little boy Mason, just a toddler then. Over the months and years which followed, they became like family to me and I even got tattoos of their names.

I was still doing the venues, talking to fans about my life, as a way of making money, even though I was pissed sometimes when I went on stage. That's when Shane Whitfield, who I have already mentioned, entered the picture, and things went from bad to worse.

Katie says she got a call from Shane in the middle of the night. "Paul's really drunk," he told her. "But don't worry. I'm going to be his agent now. We're taking him to Leicester, we'll pay for him to go to rehab."

As a young lass, trying her best to take care of me, Katie thought it was great at the time, we both did. We hoped I'd get sober, and make more money than I had done with Terry and Freda, and to begin with, it seemed like Shane had my best interests at heart. He got on well with Katie and he'd take me to football, and to play tennis.

But I never went to rehab, instead Shane took me to a fucking barn in the countryside, in the middle of nowhere. Don't get me wrong, it was a pretty nice barn, as far as barns go. It had been converted into accommodation, and it was much more comfortable than the flat I'd been living in, but I was completely isolated there and had never felt more alone. Far from getting me sober, Shane regularly dropped off alcohol, probably because I can be a difficult bastard at times, and it was the easiest way of getting me to do what he wanted.

I was still managing to do the speaking events – I was Shane's cash cow so he made sure of that. Sitting in his car one afternoon, on the way to a venue, I was pretty out of it as he pulled over and told me: "Wait here. I won't be long."

I watched as he walked up to a scruffy looking guy on the side of the road and handed him a small package. Glancing shiftily about him, the man gave Shane something in return, before quickly striding away.

"What was all that about?" I asked him, when he came back to the car.

"Just a bit of business," he said, casually.

I was too miserable to care much about what was going on around me, but it was clear Shane was messed up in something dodgy. He always seemed to be meeting dubious looking characters on street corners, and he often appeared stressed out, like he was watching his back. I was desperate to get away from him, but I didn't know how.

While I was living in the barn in Leicester, I didn't have much contact with Katie, and I missed her dreadfully. I didn't realise that Shane had changed my mobile phone number, which meant she couldn't get in touch with me. I hadn't heard from her in a few months and I wondered if I had done something to piss her off.

Usually she rang all the time and I was worried, but because of the state I was in, I just left it. However, eventually, I was concerned enough to ring her up.

"Katie, why haven't you called me?" I asked her. "Have you fallen out with me?"

"No," she said. "I just haven't been able to get through to you."

Speaking to Katie gave me a boost, and, somehow, I managed to sober up and pull myself together a bit. I had another reason to clean up my act as I'd been invited to take part in a Tottenham Hotspur Legends game, in March 2019, against a team of Inter Milan legends managed by Jose Mourinho.

I blinked away tears as I arrived in North London, almost 30 years since I'd last played for Spurs. The match was a test event for the brand new Tottenham Hotspur Stadium, which had been built on the site of White Hart Lane, a ground that held so many happy memories for me.

I was emotional, nervous and excited, thinking of all the amazing times I'd had with the club, when I played with them between 1988 and 1992, still such a young lad, and full of hope for the future.

I was 51 by this point, and not in the best of shape. Would I be able to perform?

But being back on the pitch with Robbie Keane as captain and teammates Jurgen Klinsmann, David Ginola, Dimitar Berbatov, playing against the likes of Juan Sebastian Veron and Laurent Blanc, was exhilarating. Of course, I was much slower than I had been as a lad of 21, but I like to think I managed to keep up with the rest of the old stars, none of us anywhere near as fit as we had been in our prime.

As I walked out onto the turf, the crowd went wild, chanting: "Gazza, Gazza, Gazza!" I got the biggest applause of them all, even bigger than Robbie Keane, which made me feel on the top of the world. In the end we were beaten 5-4, but it was still a brilliant experience.

Katie rang me up and told me I looked really well on the TV and I had to admit I was feeling good, better than I had in ages. In October I decided to get myself back to Bournemouth for a little holiday with Katie, and her family.

Sitting on the beach at Sandbanks, while Mason paddled in the sea, and Katie's baby, Nancie, gurgled contentedly in her arms, I felt happier than I had in a long time. Katie's husband was grilling meat on a disposable barbecue when I decided to nip to the shop to pick up a paper. I opened it up as I walked along, looking forward to a sausage sandwich when I got back, only for my appetite to disappear completely.

In the middle of the paper, there was a picture of me with Shane Whitfield, and a double page spread, the headline announcing: "GAZZA'S MANAGER CHARGED WITH DRUG DEALING."

When I got back to the beach I was in a state of shock, and couldn't bring myself to speak. Eventually, I managed to say: "The dodgy bastard. I haven't even done anything, and look, here I am in the paper!"

I held it up for Katie and Matt to see. Katie was absolutely fuming. "I trusted him to look after you," she said. "I feel so completely betrayed."

The truth was, we both did.

I went really quiet on that beach, wondering what the hell I was going to do. I hadn't been happy with Shane for a while, and I knew he'd been up to something, but I'd never expected this. What would I do without an agent? I needed to carry on doing my speaking events in order to earn money, to live.

We learnt the full scale of what Shane had been up to when he pleaded guilty to conspiracy to supply class A and B drugs and producing cannabis at Leicester Crown Court in March 2020. He'd been part of a sophisticated criminal operation involving 22 other people, who flooded Leicester with class A drugs. He was banged up for a total of 12 years, a long time by anybody's estimation.

"What am I going to do now?" I asked Katie. "I need someone to look after me, get me jobs. Who can I trust after this?"

I kept thinking about how David Beckham's physio, David Byrne, had ended up becoming his agent, because of the trust that had developed between them during the 1998 World Cup.

I'd always had issues with trust and agents in the past, but I already trusted Katie with my life. Katie at that point was on maternity leave and had most recently been working in sales. I'd seen her doing bits of work around the house, and I knew she was good at it. It's not a huge leap, from sales to being an agent and I thought it was the best idea I'd ever had.

"Katie, why don't you be my manager? Why don't you learn to be my agent? You'll pick it up really easily," I told her.

She blinked, clearly taken aback, thinking it through.

"OK," she eventually said. "Why not?"

I took her to Curry's, bought her a laptop, and started introducing her to people in the business. However, as she'd been my close friend for five years, she already knew a lot of them anyway.

Katie came with me to some of the venues I was speaking at and though we argued at times – she can be a bossy bitch – she picked things up really quickly.

By the time she'd been working for me for three months, she'd got me so many jobs I had to say: "Katie, will you slow down a bit." She works with 12 former footballers now including Vinnie Jones, Paul Merson and John Terry. Tyson Fury even calls her up for work.

I tell her: "I won't be here forever, you need to think of your future."

Five years later, Katie and I are like family. She's the first person I call in any emergency and she's always there for me. It took me more than three decades, but I now finally have an agent I can trust with my life, and I will always be grateful for that.

6

JIMMY FIVE BELLIES

I WAS IN THE DUNSTON EXCELSIOR, MY LOCAL, where I'd often go with my dad or a lass at the time for a few drinks, when a fat lad came up to me and said: "Are you Paul Gascoigne? Can I be your friend?"

"What the fuck do you mean? Can you be my friend? Are you five?" I replied.

I recognised the fella because we'd both been to the same schools – Breckenbeds Junior High School and then Heathfield. He was a few years older than me, so we were never in the same class, but I knew who he was.

I was used to all kinds of people approaching me and saying mad things as by then I was already making appearances for Newcastle United, and any chance I got, I was out nightclubbing in the city with my mates.

I looked at the lad again, he was a pudgy little chap with a cheeky grin on his face and all of a sudden I had an idea.

"Can you drive?" I asked him.

"Yes, mate," he said. "I can."

"Have you got a car?" I enquired.

"I have, yes," the lad replied.

"In that case, yes, you can be my friend," I told him.

Up until that point I'd been getting a bus or a taxi all the way from Dunston to the Newcastle training ground in Benwell, in the west end of the city, which was a pain in the arse. If this fella, Jimmy Gardner, was up for giving me a lift, then I felt sure we could be mates.

The first day Jimmy turned up to take me to the training ground, I decided to tell him a bit of a fib.

"I passed my test, you know," I said. "Is it OK if I drive the car?"

Trusting as anything, he handed me the keys, but five minutes later I'd managed to smash the vehicle into a brick wall. It didn't put Jimmy off and I learnt how to drive in that car, which was his dad's, with lots of scrapes along the way.

Jimmy was roughly the same height as me, but about 30 stone heavier, and he looked hilarious. I gave him the nickname "Five Bellies" as soon as we started knocking about together, and it stuck.

In those days, *The Sun* newspaper had an office in Newcastle city centre and every week Jimmy and I would pop in to see the photographer. This was before my trust with the press completely broke down and the photographer, a lovely guy, would let us rifle through the pictures from the most recent Newcastle United game. We'd take all the ones that featured me, and then stick them up on the walls of the Dunston Excelsior.

I didn't have much cash back then, on account of Newcastle

United paying me a mere £25 a week. Jimmy's own dad would lend me money, which I really appreciated at the time. If ever I was struggling, Jimmy was right there, always happy to help me out.

It could be stressful at times, being a young footballer, and Jimmy acted as a kind of unofficial assistant. In return, especially once I started making more money, I always made sure I took care of him. He was by my side throughout my career, and travelled all over the world with me. He was like a brother.

Pretty much wherever I went back then, Jimmy and my dad would come too. They kept each other company and became good mates themselves.

I don't know exactly what I liked so much about Jimmy, but the fact we were both absolutely nuts probably had something to do with it. One of my favourite things to do was to play practical jokes on him and there were loads over the years.

I remember being pissed off with him once, because he was supposed to be meeting me for a drink and he didn't turn up.

I rang him up and said: "Are you coming out or what?"

"I'm tired, I'm going to bed," he told me.

I'll get my own back on him, I thought to myself.

I made my way to a pet shop, and bought a snake. I am actually petrified of snakes, so I brought along a leather glove to protect my hand when I picked it up. Then I headed to Jimmy's house, and carefully posted the snake through the letter box.

A few hours later he gave me a ring. "I've woken up to a fucking snake in the house!" he cried, while I laughed my head off.

On another occasion, Jimmy was desperate to come and watch me play in Italy.

"No problem," I told him. "I'll sort your tickets. All you need to do is go and pick them up."

Well, I got him a flight from Newcastle to London to Paris to Copenhagen to Rome. The entire trip took him three days and the poor sod was absolutely furious with me by the time he arrived.

Another time, Jimmy came along to training with me as usual, just after I'd bought myself a brand new Range Rover.

"Can I have a go in your car while you train?" he asked me.

"No," I said. "You'll only crash it."

"Go on," Jimmy begged. "Please, please, I've always wanted to drive a Range Rover."

"All right, then," I replied.

As Jimmy shot off I rang the police and said: "My car's been stolen."

A short time later, poor old Jimmy was pulled over by an officer.

"I'm Paul's best friend," he pleaded. "He's given me permission to drive his car."

The cops called me up and said: "Do you know a Jimmy Gardner?"

"I've never heard of him in my life," I said, pissing myself.

There was one time Jimmy got into trouble with the law for real, when some young lads started yelling "fat bastard" at him in the street just after he'd picked up a Chinese takeaway in Gateshead.

He'd been out drinking, but I think he'd only had about five pints, and had nipped to get the food when the youngsters started taking the piss out of his famous belly. Jimmy had been on a diet, so hadn't had a drink for a while, and the booze had gone to his head a bit.

It's not nice being called fat. Don't get me wrong, I was always making jibes about Jimmy's weight myself but as I was his best mate he didn't let it get to him.

I can understand why Jimmy snapped and went home to get his air pistol, which wasn't even loaded. Unfortunately, as he was roaming the streets looking for the lads who'd upset him, only meaning to give them a fright, he was spotted by the police. He ended up pleading guilty to charges of possession of an air pistol with intent to cause fear of violence and did four weeks in prison.

Jimmy had always been incredibly loyal to me, but unfortunately we fell out badly over a story in the papers about 14 years ago. I was fuming at the time, as we'd been close for so long. That was our friendship over. A lot of time has passed now – he's moved on, so have I. It's sad, but that's life.

2 JOY

PROLOGUE

JOY – A feeling of great pleasure or happiness that comes from success, good fortune or a sense of well-being.

I AM FEELING A BIT DEPRESSED, DOWN IN THE dumps, which happens sometimes, now I live alone. It's all too easy to pick up a drink in these situations, but instead, I force myself to leave my flat. It's an ordinary day in Poole, let's call it a Tuesday, but as I walk through the streets there are cries of "Gazza!", "legend", "hero", while fans run up to me, asking for a selfie.

If I am feeling bad about myself, all I have to do is get out and about and I am reminded how much the public still loves me. It's mad, but for some reason, I am just as recognisable now as I was when I was at the height of my career. So, that brings me a fair amount of joy, knowing I was that good at football, people haven't forgotten, all these years later.

I was in Bournemouth once, struggling down the road with an ironing board, a microwave and an iron I'd bought for a new flat. I was making my way slowly to the taxi I'd booked, puffing and panting, when this guy yelled: "Gazza! Gazza! Can I have a selfie?" Fucking hell, I thought to myself, as I put everything down, posed with the lad, then picked it all back up again.

It took me about 45 minutes, but the words of my dad are always ringing in my ears when this kind of thing happens. "Never forget where you came from," and I haven't. I don't mind really, no matter how inconvenient it is, as my fans have become like family to me now and I love them as much as they love me.

Something else which brings me a lot of joy is helping other people, and seeing them happy, as I get really depressed sometimes, thinking about how much misery there is in the world.

I said to my dad once: "Why doesn't the Government just print billions and billions and billions and make everyone a billionaire?"

He replied: "Are you daft, son, or what? Have you heard of inflation? Besides, imagine, if everything was perfect, life would be so fucking boring. You wouldn't get to enjoy the good bits."

Maybe he was right, but if I see someone struggling or in pain, I will do everything I can to help them, I've always been like that. I've been lucky enough to earn millions during my time as a footballer and sharing that money has brought me no end of joy.

Being able to help my family, buy them houses, cars and take them on holiday, has been one of the greatest pleasures of my life.

What I never take for granted is the life I have built for

myself here, in Poole, with Katie, and her family. I open my eyes in the morning, and most of the time I'm sober, which is the best feeling in the world.

There are no hazy memories of the night before and I don't have to try to work out where I have been, who I have pissed off or what important item I have lost – keys, bank cards, phone. That's bliss.

I stay in Katie's spare room sometimes, and I love being with her kids, especially her daughter, Nancie.

"Uncle Gazza," she said to me the other day. "Are you alright?"

"Yeah, I'm alreet, Nancie. I am going to the dentist today, do you know what time I'm going?"

"No," she replied.

"Tooth-thirty," I told her.

"Tooth-thirty, tooth-hurty," she said, over and over again, while both of us struggled to breathe, we were laughing that much. I love spending time with kids, probably because I am still a kid myself, at heart.

Of course, I have experienced some of my most intense joys on the football pitch, and for a very long time, that's what I lived for. It didn't matter what kind of shit was going on in my personal life, for 90 minutes nothing else mattered, I was free from all of my dark thoughts, the OCD, the anxiety, it disappeared. Those days are behind me now, and I have to appreciate the joys of my new life, without football.

I've loved fishing since I was a lad, it's what I've always done to relax, and it still helps to clear my mind, and focus my thoughts. Sitting on the banks of the river, all alone, waiting for the fish to bite, is a joy of its own.

I've just bought a David Lloyd membership for me and Katie

and her kids, as I also love going to the gym, when I am fit enough. When I am sober and in a good place, I will often be sweating my arse off on the treadmill, then I will go on the cross trainer, and maybe finish with weights – I don't know when to stop. I have to be careful as I get obsessed with things very easily and take them to the extreme. I'm just going to the sauna for now, because if I go into the gym, that will be it. I take it too far and end up in agony.

When I was younger, alcohol brought me a lot of joy, and for a short while, cocaine did as well. But that joy always came at a steep price. The joys I experience today are quieter, not as intense, but they bring me peace, where once they tore my life apart, and I am grateful for that.

1

NEWCASTLE UNITED FIRST TEAM

HOW I LOVED THE ROTHMAN'S FOOTBALL Yearbook. Back in the day, before the internet, it was considered the bible of football – essential reading for every fan, filled with facts, figures and reports on all the clubs in the league.

One day, during training, the Newcastle manager, Willie McFaul, called me into his office.

"I've just received an advance copy," he told me, hugging the 1986/87 edition to his chest.

"Guess who's on the front?" he asked, holding it up for me to see.

"No way!" I exclaimed.

There I was, a fat bastard, giving Liverpool defender Mark Lawrenson a proper shove. It wasn't a very flattering image, this chubby kid with a mass of hair, appearing to elbow a legend of the game in the face, but for a lad who had just completed his first full season in the first team, it was absolutely brilliant.

I was only 19, but already my time at Newcastle had been filled with drama. From the moment I walked through the door as a schoolboy in 1980, the club was in a constant state of flux. The manager at the time, Bill McGarry, left within a month, replaced by Arthur Cox – a sergeant major type of character, who I loved, loathed and feared in equal measure. Under Cox, the club finally started going places after languishing in Division Two. Like I said earlier, the turning point came in 1982 when he somehow persuaded Kevin Keegan, twice voted European Footballer of the Year, to step down a division and come and play for us. For a Newcastle fan, it was beyond our wildest dreams.

As part of my apprenticeship chores, I got to look after Keegan's boots. It was something trainees always did back then – clean the boots of the senior pros as well as sweep the floors, scrub the toilets, and make cups of tea for the first team squad. We'd then have to wash the communal baths, clean the cups the players had been drinking from, and pick up their dirty kit. When we were allowed to have a bath after training, we had to use the same water the first team had bathed in. Disgusting, when you think about it. Very little time was actually spent with a ball at our feet.

Anyway, I couldn't wait to show Kevin's boots off to my mates on the bus home. "These, my friends, are the boots of King Kev, the Messiah," I told them, passing them around. They were well impressed and I was in my element – that was, until I got home.

With a feeling of absolute dread, I realised I only had one boot – the other had vanished.

"Dad!" I shouted. "Shit! I've lost Kevin Keegan's boot!"

My dad was brilliant, and contacted the bus depot while I prayed it would be found. Unfortunately, there was no sign of it anywhere, and I knew I had no choice but to come clean.

I was absolutely shitting myself about telling Kevin, and was convinced I was going to be sacked. But instead of bollocking me, he burst out laughing. "Don't worry about it," he told me. "It's not the end of the world."

I'd never been so relieved in my life.

Kevin Keegan was a real inspiration to everyone at the club. I'll never forget how, on his first day, he waved and smiled at all the apprentices. He brought a sense of fun back to the place and occasionally, he would share his advice.

"Demand the ball," he'd tell me. "Don't be afraid to take charge of a game."

Kevin led the club to promotion to Division One in the 1983/84 season, ably assisted by the likes of Chris Waddle, Peter Beardsley and Terry McDermott. The fans were so proud of the team, they even wrote a song about them. It was called 'Goin' Up' by Busker, and I would sing it all the time. "Look out Hoddle, we've got Waddle / When he takes players on it's one big doddle / New boy Peter runs like a cheetah / Beardsley's going to be a world beater." During the height of Gazzamania in 1990, when Radio 5 first launched, they asked me to select my favourite songs for a special Christmas broadcast, and this tune was right at the top of the list.

The only disappointment of that season was when Keegan decided to retire. He knew he couldn't perform to the best of his abilities any longer and wanted to go out on a high. His last game was a 2-2 draw against Liverpool and afterwards, he made a grand exit in a helicopter. A certain Alan Shearer was a ball boy that night, and he looked on in wonder.

Meanwhile, I was being put through my paces by our youth team coach, Colin Suggett. He would make me run endlessly, lap after lap of the training pitch, to help keep my weight down, and it was Suggett who first called me Gazza – his Sunderland accent mangling my occasional nickname of Gassa. I struggled with the fitness side of training, but whenever a ball was involved my skills shone through. We sometimes did activities in the gym with the first team, and it would involve shooting a ball through a shape – a triangle, square, circle – randomly called out by the coach. Normally, I was the only apprentice there able to succeed in the challenge, and it made people like Chris Waddle take notice of me. "Maybe he isn't just a lazy fat shit after all," he probably thought.

I was desperate to turn professional when my two-year apprenticeship was up, so I endured Suggett's constant moans about my weight, my diet, and my fitness, and I carried on running more laps than any of the other players. I even put in additional work to improve my upper body strength, using weights to make myself stronger, which proved useful when I started playing with the older pros as they all had a really hard time knocking me off the ball. As a youngster, along with my ball skills, this trait made me stand out as someone a bit different.

Hot on the heels of Kevin Keegan's departure, Arthur Cox left too after he had a row with the board over the direction the club was taking. I had a lot of respect for him, even though he once gave me a bollocking just for touching the team sheet! Another time, he made me take away a cup of tea I'd made for him, just because I'd touched the rim with my fingers. When I brought back a freshly made brew, he waved me away saying: "I've changed my mind, I don't want it now."

Jack Charlton, the 1966 World Cup winner born and bred in Ashington, Northumberland, took over as manager, and although he was quite brutal in his treatment, giving me two weeks to lose weight or else I'd be sacked, the 1984/85 season saw me flourish as captain of the youth team. In April 1985 Jack gave me my first-team debut, as substitute at home to Queens Park Rangers, which ended in a 1-0 win. Soon afterwards he told me the news I'd been longing to hear – I was to be given a two-year contract as a professional footballer.

By the start of the 1985/86 season, we had yet another new manager in charge. The supporters had been chanting for Jack to be sacked, and he'd taken this to heart. "I don't need this," I heard him say during one pre-season match, and before you knew it, he had gone. He was replaced by Willie McFaul, who I had known since I signed as a schoolboy. Chris Waddle had also left, underlining the basic truth that Newcastle were a selling club, but at least we still had Peter Beardsley.

Peter was great with me while I was making my way into the first team squad. He would give me £5 from his own wages, saying: "Don't tell my wife about this." He once lent me £80 for a pair of shoes – a lot of money back then – and never asked for the cash back.

I also had the support of the first team captain Glenn Roeder, who I knew I could always go to for advice or help when needed. Glenn was a Londoner with a great sense of style, and he used to wear a full-length sheepskin coat right down to his ankles, which I adored. One time, when he got on a bus with a bunch of us apprentices, I asked if I could wear it if I carried his bag for him. He was far taller and thinner than me, and the coat almost swallowed me up!

The new season started well for me as I took Waddle's place in the first XI. The excitement of playing for Newcastle was intoxicating, I wasn't interested in tracking back or being disciplined, I just wanted to take the opposition on single-handed. We earned three victories, including a 1-0 win over Liverpool, and two draws from our first five matches, but then we got hammered 3-0 by Manchester United at Old Trafford. I was left out of the side for the following away game to Spurs, which we lost 5-1. I came on as a substitute near the end and was made up when I heard the crowd chanting my name.

Two games later, I managed to score my first goal for Newcastle in a 3-0 win over Oxford United and, injuries aside, was able to stay in the team for most of the season, making 35 appearances and scoring nine goals. There were times when I was overwhelmed by pleasure and excitement at coming face to face with some of my heroes.

Playing against Liverpool at Anfield, I sidled up to their player-manager Kenny Dalglish while waiting for a corner kick to be taken. "Alreet, Kenny?" I asked him, much to his bemusement. And when Manchester United came to St James' Park near the end of the season and my hero Bryan Robson scored from the penalty spot as they defeated us 4-2, I was unable to hide my admiration. As he ran back to restart the game, I told him: "Great penalty, Bryan!"

That summer, Peter Beardsley went off to the 1986 World Cup in Mexico, and made a name for himself with some great displays. It made me realise what was possible – if he could go and do that while playing for Newcastle United, then maybe in a few years I could too. I also knew that Newcastle were a selling club, so Peter probably wouldn't stay for too much longer. I was right, and in 1987, he was sold to Liverpool for £1.9million. The 1986/87 season was a struggle, we were in a relegation scrap for a long time and by the end of February we were five points adrift at the bottom of the table. I missed a lot of games through injury, but my return to the side coincided with an upturn in results. With the help of Paul Goddard's goals we managed to climb up to 17th position and safety. I was pleased enough with my form when I did play, and my displays earned me a call-up to the England Under 21 squad – my first international recognition.

Peter's departure to Liverpool, for a British record fee, led to Newcastle signing the Brazilian striker Mirandinha as his replacement in a £575,000 transfer from Palmeiras. It was a bold move, very few foreign players plied their trade in England at that time, and certainly not many Brazilians! He had impressed when Brazil had played England in a Rous Cup game at Wembley in May 1987, scoring their equaliser in a 1-1 draw. The two of us developed a great partnership, on and off the pitch. When he first arrived, all the players lined up at the training ground to shake his hand. As soon as I greeted him, I darted to the end of the line to do it again, wondering if he would notice. I also took it upon myself to teach him some essential English words, everyday phrases that he would need to know, like "fuck off," "piss off" and "why aye, man". He would have all the lads in stitches by referring to Wednesday as "Wankday".

From the moment he made his debut, away at Norwich

City, the fans took him to their hearts, wearing sombreros and chanting: "We've got Mirandinha, he's not from Argentina, he's from Brazil, he's fucking brill!" They loved how he would shoot from any position on the field, sometimes as far away as 60 yards. I should have taught him the word "pass," as he never gave the ball to anyone else. We formed a close bond, despite the language barrier, going to charity events together and meeting each other's families. His children were desperate for a dog, so I bought them a springer spaniel. As a way of saying thanks, Mira called the dog Gazza.

Things were going well on the pitch, even though St James' Park looked like a building site. We had to use portacabins as makeshift dressing rooms while a new stand was constructed. I won the Barclays Young Eagle of the Month award for October and I was a rising star in the league, as well as a mainstay of the Newcastle side. Manchester United came to St James' Park on Boxing Day 1987 and I played a blinder against Bryan Robson, as we beat them 1-0. Robbo later told me how Alex Ferguson had a right go at him at half time. "Any chance you could get a fucking tackle in on Gascoigne?" Fergie bawled. "I'm trying gaffer," Robbo replied, "but he's not a bad player, you know."

By the new year, my form was unstoppable. We played Spurs on a mudbath of a pitch at St James' Park towards the end of January 1988, and after picking up another Young Eagle of the Month award before the game, I impressed their new manager Terry Venables by scoring twice in a 2-0 win. "At least you're wearing the right boots," he told me afterwards, noticing they were Hummel, who sponsored Tottenham's kit. He later said my performance was one of the finest he had ever seen by a young player.

EIGHT

The following week, Bobby Robson was watching from the stands as Newcastle romped to a 5-0 FA Cup win over Swindon Town, and I was hoping I'd made a good impression on the England manager. It turned out to be a good season, which also saw us defeat Liverpool on penalties at Wembley in the Mercantile Credit Football Festival. But by that point I knew other teams were showing an interest in me, and the club displayed no ambition in their outlook. They had sold Waddle and Beardsley and I made it known that I would not be signing a new contract and was looking to leave. It was just a question of where I wanted to go. My preference was Liverpool, who were the best team in the country by far, but they could not afford to sign me at that point. So it came down to Manchester United or Spurs.

The transfer speculation did affect my game at the time. In April 1988, I got sent off at Derby County, managed by my old boss Arthur Cox, and afterwards I trashed the away dressing room. My behaviour was so bad, I actually wrote a letter to Arthur apologising for my conduct. One week later, I was awarded the 1987/88 PFA Young Player of the Year trophy, presented to me by one of my heroes, Bobby Charlton.

My final game for Newcastle was against West Ham at St James' Park, the last match of the season, which we won 2-1. Nothing had been settled by that point, but it was clear I would not be at Newcastle the following season. At the end of the game I applauded the fans in the stadium, and said some quiet farewells to a few players in the dressing room. It was a low-key way to end my long association with the club I loved, but I had to leave, for the good of my career.

The following season, the club splashed out on a glut of new players, spending the £2.2million they'd got for me on Dave Beasant, Andy Thorn, John Robertson, and John Hendrie. Excitement was high on Tyneside, but within a few months Willie McFaul had been sacked, and the team were relegated at the end of the season, finishing bottom of the league.

ENGLAND DEBUT

To Sir Bobby from Daft as a Brush

When I was 12 I met a man called Bobby,
It was in Ipswich in a lobby,
At first I seen him he just smiled with such glee,
I knew he was the man for me,
He was a great man,
Even better than Peter Pan,
He looked after me for so many years,
He was like a tree with the fruit of the pears,
I know he's above,
And I'll always be his son like the feathers of a dove,
He has now passed away,
But every night I say a little pray,
For the great man Sir Bobby he will be missed,
*I've kept okay and hope not to get p****d*

I will never forget you for as long as I live,
You gave me a chance,
I started to bounce,
There are no rules for loving and sharing,
But hearts beat faster when someone is caring.

Love Gazza

I hope you like this poem I wrote, and feel it does justice to the great man Sir Bobby Robson, my friend and mentor. Out of all the players and managers I have had the privilege of working alongside throughout my footballing career, Bobby is the one I loved and respected the most. He was like a second father to me, and I was devastated when he died in 2009, aged 76.

I think part of the reason I felt such affinity for Bobby was because, like me, he was a son of the North East, born in Sacriston, County Durham, in 1933. He'd also played in the same position of attacking midfielder while at Fulham, West Bromwich Albion and England in the 1950s.

When I was just 12 years old I went down to Ipswich with Keith Spraggon for my first ever trial. Bobby was the manager, and I warmed to him immediately, although I think that was partly to do with the fact he was the only one down there able to understand what I was saying in my thick Geordie accent.

I'll never forget him telling the young lads: "Most of you won't make it, but don't let that get you down. It's an achievement just to be here."

I didn't manage to impress Bobby, so the trial didn't lead to anything, but he mustn't have forgotten it, as years later he remembered me as a "fat little boy" in his autobiography.

Bobby became the manager of England in 1982, the year before I signed for Newcastle. It was the most prestigious job in football, but also the most stressful. I must have been on Bobby's radar from 1987 onwards, as by then I was playing for the England Under 21s, managed by Dave Sexton, but I didn't make it to the full squad until September 1988 following my move to Spurs.

Bobby had selected me for a friendly against Denmark, and I managed to get onto the pitch with just a few minutes remaining, replacing Peter Beardsley to make my England debut. I must have only touched the ball twice at most, but I was just happy to have won my first England cap at the age of 21.

I was chosen for the next few squads, but made no further appearances. I enjoyed it nevertheless, and learned a lot. Poor Bobby was getting vile abuse from the media at that time as we had gone into the 1988 European Championship as one of the favourites to win, but ended up losing all three games we played. From then on, the press were out to get him. By the time we travelled to Saudi Arabia in November, the criticism had become completely over the top. We drew 1-1 in a friendly with the Saudis only to come home to headlines of: "In the Name of Allah, Go." Lesser men would have walked away, but Bobby was brave and he stuck it out. He was a true patriot and it would have broken his heart to leave. At the time I was more disappointed about missing out on a brand new Ford XR3i Cabriolet car, which all the players who started the game against the Saudis had been promised. I did, however, make my second England appearance in that match, coming on with just five minutes remaining and little chance of making an impression.

Although I wasn't being given many opportunities on the

pitch, I was starting to feel like a squad regular by the time we visited Albania, in February 1989. There wasn't much to do over there, and we were practically confined to our hotel, which had no facilities to speak of. The only form of entertainment I found was to throw bars of soap at the chickens in the yard below my hotel window. My roommate Chris Waddle joined in, and so we laid bets on who could hit the most birds. I had just managed to land a bullseye, hitting one of the chickens dead on with the soap, when over my shoulder I saw Bobby Robson standing there. "What are you up to?" he asked, with a bemused look on his face. "We're throwing bars of soap at the chickens," I said. He gave a laugh and walked away. Off the pitch we were behaving like childish idiots, but we still managed to beat the Albanians 2-0.

When we next faced Albania, at Wembley in April, the country was still in mourning following the Hillsborough disaster, which had happened only 11 days earlier. The world of football was at its lowest ebb, and badly needed a lift. Thankfully we romped to a 5-0 victory, and I scored my first goal for England. I came on with 24 minutes of the game remaining when the score was 3-0 in our favour, but I desperately wanted to make an impression. Bobby had asked me to play wide on the right, but in my excitement I forgot all about his tactical instructions and chased the ball as if I was a schoolboy in the playground. Luckily, it went well for me, and I was able to create a fourth goal for Chris Waddle, before hitting the back of the net myself with a mazy dribble and shot from inside the penalty box.

The crowd went home singing my name, the commentators described me as a star of the future, but Bobby Robson didn't share their enthusiasm. He slaughtered me after the match for disobeying his instructions, and he told the media we had needed two balls – "One for Gascoigne and another for the rest of the team." But there was a twinkle in his eye as he said it, and he also described me as "a precocious and rare talent" so I knew deep down he had quite enjoyed my performance.

I could understand him wanting to keep my feet on the ground, and I guess that is where his famous "Daft as a Brush" description of me came from. I didn't take it seriously, but he clearly saw me as an ill-disciplined joker. He first made that comment as an aside to coach Dave Sexton during the Albania game, but he then repeated it to the media before another match a few months later. Did I take his comments on board? Well, the day after he said it, I came out to training with a carpet brush down my sock. Even Bobby had to laugh at that.

He did have some unconventional ways of making a point, did Bobby. We played Sweden away in a World Cup qualifier, in September 1989, and Terry Butcher took an awful cut to the head. I was on the substitutes bench, and when Terry went off to get stitched up in the dressing room, Bobby asked me to go along as well. I couldn't understand why – what could I do to help? When Terry came back onto the pitch, I made my way to the England bench. "That," Bobby said to me, "is what it means to represent your country." By the end of the game, Terry's white shirt had turned red with blood. I played the final 20 minutes, and earned a "well done" from the manager, even though I had done nothing spectacular – just kept things tight, as he had asked me to.

It wasn't until we played a friendly against Czechoslovakia in April 1990 that I felt confident about being picked for the Italia '90 squad. That was my coming of age game – I needed to play well in that match to be certain of going to Italy, and after a nervous first 20 minutes I turned in one of the best performances of my career. I had a hand in creating three of our goals in a 4-2 victory, and scored the fourth myself. Bobby was just as impressed by my discipline when he played me against Denmark in the next match, and he then gave me one final test against Uruguay, a team historically renowned for their dirty tricks and cynical behaviour. Although we lost that game 2-1, Bobby had viewed it as a test of my temperament, and he was pleased with how I'd handled myself against a difficult side.

By that point I had proven myself as a player Bobby could rely upon to carry out a job in the centre of midfield, as well as someone able to provide a spark of creativity further forward. My place in the squad for the 1990 World Cup had been confirmed and the stage was set for me to take the tournament by storm.

Being in the England team meant the world to me, as I'd been shitting myself about making the squad in the first place. It was touch and go whether Bobby Robson would pick me, right up until we played Czechoslovakia at Wembley, four weeks before he named his squad.

This was a make or break game for me. If I messed things up, my chances of going to Italy for the World Cup were nil, so I was absolutely horrified when the Czechs got an early goal. Thankfully, it put a bit of a rocket up my arse and I managed to pass to Steve Bull who volleyed the ball into the back of the net.

After that, I couldn't put a foot wrong – a few minutes later, I set up a goal for Stuart Pearce from a corner kick, and then provided the cross for Bull to score another, making it easy for him to head home from close range. Best of all, I claimed the fourth goal for myself, finding the energy to run into the box in the final moments of the game and smash the ball into the net.

"Yes! Get in!" I screamed, running along the pitch with my hands in the air, feeling more alive than ever.

While I was celebrating, the TV cameras picked up Bobby Robson wagging his finger and saying: "That was fantastic." Once I saw that, I knew for certain I'd made the squad, and I was absolutely elated.

3

WORLD CUP '90

"I'M DONE FOR," I THOUGHT, AS I TURNED AWAY from the ecstatic Tunisia players, who'd just scored a spectacular goal. I had meant to pass the ball to Gary Stevens but it took a bobble on the awful pitch and instead, it ended up with Abdelhamid Hergal.

Before I had time to process what was happening the Tunisian had lobbed the ball over our goalkeeper Peter Shilton and into the back of the net from 40 yards away, easy as anything, and the African fans went wild. No-one expected Tunisia to score first in a game against England, but that's what happened and it was all my fault. I was absolutely devastated.

We were playing a friendly in the baking heat of Charguia at the Stade Olympique El Menzah ahead of the 1990 World Cup. Luckily, Steve Bull managed to score an equaliser in the 89th minute, so the match ended 1-1, but that was no thanks to me, and I was convinced I no longer had any hope of playing in the tournament. We would be playing our first World Cup match in just nine days' time.

But afterwards, manager Bobby Robson, who was always decent towards me, even when I fucked up, put his hand on my shoulder and told me not to worry. I was still just a lad of 23 and he knew I had a tendency to behave like a daft bastard at times.

He told me: "You are staying next to me, I am keeping an eye on you throughout this whole World Cup."

"I won't let you down," I replied.

However, despite the quality of my football, it was far from plain sailing before I boarded that flight to Italy and there were a fair few mishaps along the way.

I travelled up to Gateshead to say goodbye to my family and friends, and I'll admit I had a few drinks. We were all so excited ahead of the tournament, I suppose I got carried away. A bit worse for wear, I ended up in a skirmish with another lad in Newcastle city centre and the cops arrested me outside Berlins Wine Bar.

"Oh, shit," I thought. "I'm done for."

Thankfully, the police questioned me for an hour then let me go without charge – it was the longest hour of my life.

My head must have been all over the place as I made my way back down south to prepare for the journey to Italy. I started to pack but then with horror, I realised I'd left my passport behind. We were due to fly from Luton Airport the very next day, and there simply wasn't enough time for me to drive to Gateshead and back to get it.

"Fuck!" I yelled, then tried to calm down so I could think.

I rang Jimmy, who'd been getting me out of these kinds of scrapes since I was a kid, and asked: "Any chance you could go to my mam's, get my passport, then drive down to London?"

"Fucking hell," he replied. "I'll be driving all fucking night."

But he did it, of course he did it – my friends and family would have done anything to make sure I made it to Italy for the World Cup.

Unfortunately, the debacle outside the wine bar in Newcastle had made the papers – I'd been hitting the headlines all week, and I hadn't even left the country. When I saw the other players, they bombarded me with questions. "Are you going to sue the papers?" they asked. "Nah," I said. "I smacked the c***, didn't I?"

My problem was, I was like a little pressure cooker, ready to explode at any given moment. I had so much energy, I simply didn't know what to do with it, so while the other lads relaxed in the run up to the tournament, I'd be getting up to all sorts.

Once we got to our training camp, I remember lying next to the pool in the Is Molas resort, in southern Sardinia, gazing at the beautiful Sulcis Mountains in the distance, willing myself to stay calm and rest ahead of the first game. But it was no use, within minutes I'd jumped off my sunbed and was weaving my way through the vast hotel grounds, which were attached to a golf club, up to the room Terry Butcher shared with his Rangers teammate Chris Woods.

I rapped on the door a couple of times and ventured: "Chris? Chris?" When there was no answer I tentatively tried the handle and went inside. I headed straight for the minibar and – I know what you're thinking, but it wasn't like that – helped myself to their bars of Cadbury chocolate, slipped them into my pocket and left, smiling at the thought I now had at least three to eat – mine, Chris's and Terry's.

England's doctor John Crane was a stingy bastard and he

allowed us just one chocolate bar a day, which wasn't anywhere near enough for a sweet-toothed lad like me.

Making my getaway, all of a sudden I felt a blow to the back of my head and I went flying down the corridor. I turned around to see Terry and Chris behind me. "You're busted," Chris told me. "Give us that chocolate back, now."

It sounds so daft, like I was a kid of five or something, but it was the kind of thing I loved to do. When we weren't playing or training, I just wanted to have a laugh.

A golf day was held for the England players while we were out there, and all of us were told to dress smart as fuck and behave ourselves on the course.

"Fuck that," I thought to myself.

I was in a golf buggy with Steve McMahon and I decided to take my England top off. I knew it was against the rules, but it was a baking hot day. Steve was driving and he asked me what was coming over the hill. As I leaned out, he smacked into a tree and a branch hit me like a ton of bricks, straight across the chest. I fell from the buggy and somersaulted backwards, wearing only my shorts. When I came to a standstill and opened my eyes, Bobby Robson was staring straight at me, giving me daggers.

"Sorry, gaffer," I told him.

"Gascoigne," he barked. "Get off this golf course right now."

Despite my antics, I was on top form, and I was a first team regular throughout the tournament. By the time England played Holland in the second match of the group stage in Cagliari, I felt right at home on the big stage. I didn't care who we were up against, huge reputations never fazed me at all. I tugged on Ruud Gullit's dreadlocks during the match, and asked Ronald

Koeman how much he earned. They couldn't believe it – this daft Geordie not giving a fuck about upsetting superstars, but that was the way I was. More importantly, I was the stand-out player on the pitch and I knew it.

The game ended in a 0-0 draw, but we had played really well, employing a sweeper system for the first time to great effect, and had two goals chalked off by referee Zoran Petrović. Like I mentioned earlier, I even managed to do a Cruyff turn against Ronald Koeman – fancy, an Englishman doing that to a Dutchman! I grabbed the headlines in the days afterwards because of my performance, and in the eyes of most pundits it was the game that confirmed I was now one of the best players in the world.

Off the pitch, although I struggled to relax, I was disciplined and Bobby Robson saw a new side to me. My fitness levels surprised him, as did my diet – if I felt I was putting on a little weight, I would pass a message on to the manager through the team doctor that I would not be attending the evening meal that night, just to make sure I stayed in the best condition possible.

We made it through to the second round after defeating Egypt 1-0, thanks to a Mark Wright header from my free-kick. When we scored I raced to the touchline and started celebrating wildly, and did the same again at the final whistle. We were now at the knock-out stages, and it was such a relief.

Our next match would be against Belgium in Bologna, so we said farewell to Sardinia and hello to mainland Italy. I tried to be on my best behaviour, but I had so much pent-up energy and excitement there was absolutely no way I could go to bed and sleep like everyone else.

All the other lads were tucked up, but I decided to go for a walk around the hotel and I came across a couple of Americans. We got talking and I managed to persuade one of them to have a game of tennis with me.

It was about 11pm and we'd been playing for 20 minutes when I heard Bobby Robson shout: "Gazza, Gazza, where are you?"

I dropped my tennis racquet as quickly as anything and started legging it back to my room. As I made off I heard him asking the Americans: "Have you seen Gazza anywhere? Paul Gascoigne, the footballer?"

Luckily, being American, they had no clue who I was.

I got back to the room, jumped straight under the covers of the bed, and said to Chris: "If the gaffer knocks, tell him I am sleeping."

Seconds later, there were two sharp raps on the door and sure enough it was Bobby, come to check up on me.

"Where is he?" he asked Chris.

"He's sleeping," Chris replied.

"He's not sleeping," said Bobby. "He's just been playing tennis for 45 minutes."

Chris said: "Have you, Gazza?"

But I didn't reply, I just kept my eyes closed, and pretended I was fast asleep.

My problem was I could never relax, especially ahead of a big game, and I hated to be alone, even for five minutes. It was so bad during the World Cup that the players had a rota, each one taking their turn to spend half an hour with me. I'd play tennis with Chris Waddle, Gary Lineker would take me out on a pedalo, then I'd have a game of table tennis with Peter Beardsley.

I could have used that extra energy when we faced Belgium, as the game went into extra time and I was knackered. Belgium were a good team, and in Enzo Scifo they had a fabulous playmaker who caused us a lot of problems. But we played well, too, and with just seconds of the match remaining it looked likely that the outcome would be decided on penalty kicks.

Somehow, I managed to find an extra burst of energy as I ran towards the Belgium defence and won us a free-kick 30 yards from goal. I could hear Bobby Robson urging me to put the ball into the box, which I did perfectly, floating it into David Platt's path for him to twist and volley into the net. We'd won the game with virtually the very last kick.

The next day, we were relaxing by the pool, enjoying a day of rest ahead of our quarter-final against Cameroon in Naples. Jim Rosenthal, the ITV reporter who had been with us throughout the tournament, mistakenly thought it was my birthday, so he presented me with a huge chocolate cake in front of all the players. It didn't take long for Chris Waddle to smash the cake into my face – all I could say was: "I just love chocolate!"

We had been informed by one of our scouts, the experienced manager Howard Wilkinson, that we should have no trouble seeing off Cameroon in our next game. They had been the surprise team of the World Cup, beating Argentina in the opening match, with their 38-year-old striker Roger Milla emerging as one of the stars of the tournament. But they were missing a number of players due to suspension, and Howard said we had pretty much been given a bye into the semi-finals.

But by the end of the game, Chris Waddle was sat with Bobby Robson in the dressing room, sweat pouring off him, saying: "No more fucking byes, gaffer. That was the hardest match I've ever had!"

We had started well enough, with David Platt heading home to put us 1-0 ahead, but at half-time Bobby Robson was not happy. "Carry on like this," he said, "and we will lose this game." And he was right. Before we knew it, Cameroon had equalised when I conceded a penalty after fouling Roger Milla in the box. I honestly felt like crying at that point, I was devastated. Then Ekéké burst through to put the Africans 2-1 ahead. We were in big trouble, and I was having a shocker. With ten minutes to go, Gary Lineker won us a penalty, which he scored to make it 2-2, taking the game into extra time. And, once again, somehow I found the energy to make the decisive pass for Lineker to win us another penalty. He smashed the ball straight into the net – it was 3-2 and we managed to hold out until the end. It was a brilliant result for us, though it was hard won – all these years later I still maintain we showed more courage and heart than in any other game.

We were now set to face West Germany in the World Cup semi-final – the first time we had ever reached that stage on foreign soil.

The morning of the semi-final in Turin, Bobby Robson collared me and said: "Today, you are playing against the best midfield player in the world, Lothar Matthaus, the West German captain."

"Gaffer," I said, "Don't you worry. You smoke your cigar and relax, I can handle him."

True to my word, I performed well on the pitch that evening, we all did. West Germany had been the best team in the tournament up until then, but we outplayed them over 90 minutes and as we headed into extra time the score stood at 1-1. That's when it all went wrong for me. I was heading towards the touchline with the ball when I took a bit of a heavy touch, and Thomas Berthold managed to get it off me. I lunged towards him in a bid to reclaim the ball, but as I did so, my right foot must have just caught him.

Over he went, hitting the turf like a ton of bricks as though I had walloped him, which I hadn't. He was no real threat on the pitch, I just wanted to get the ball back. But he was really going for it, Berthold, rolling over and over, as though I'd tried to kill him or something, and I thought the ref might deem it a foul. I immediately put my hands in the air in surrender and I went over to Berthold, who was still writhing around on the floor, to show it was an accident and I'd meant nothing by it.

He was squealing like a pig, so I tried to stick my fingers in his mouth to shut him up. Then, I saw it – the yellow card, which signalled the end of my World Cup dreams. I'd already picked up a booking earlier in the tournament against Belgium, so this meant I wouldn't be playing in the final, should we get there, due to suspension.

I stood on the pitch, heartbroken, as the crowd roared and Gary Lineker gently put his hand on my arm. I turned away from him, too upset to say anything.

My bottom lip was trembling, and I just couldn't help it. I started to weep, but not out of devastation, like most people assume. I was only 23 years old and I'd never experienced joy like the World Cup. I'd had an absolute blast with my mates, and on some level I think I realised that life wouldn't get any better than this.

My emotions hit me at once, possibly all eight of them, and

I was just totally overwhelmed. But I think I was crying more out of joy, and the love of the game, than sadness – even though it was all over for me.

Despite this, I knew that I had to give it my absolute all for the rest of the game, so I tried to pull myself together. We played well, but didn't manage to score and in the end, it all came down to penalties. I was supposed to take one, but I was far too worked up, and so David Platt claimed the kick that should have been mine.

Platt scored but Chris Waddle and Stuart Pearce missed, meaning that was it, it was all over. We'd played spectacularly, but we were out of the tournament and I was in floods of tears for a second time.

Bobby Robson put his arm around me and said: "You've been one of the best players of the tournament. Don't worry, son. Don't worry, son. You've been absolutely magnificent. You've got your life ahead of you. This is your first."

He was like a father to me, the gaffer, and I clung to his words. "There'll be other World Cups," I told myself, but I was in bits.

In the aftermath of the shoot-out defeat, as the Germans celebrated and we stood there dazed, Terry Butcher came up and consoled me. My tears were still flowing freely but he guided me over to the England fans and we raised our arms to applaud our heartbroken supporters. I kissed my shirt and waved at them – the gesture became one of the defining images of Italia '90.

There were even more tears in the dressing room afterwards. It had been a heartbreaking way to lose the game, and poor Stuart Pearce and Chris Waddle were inconsolable. What could you say to them? They felt responsible for our defeat, but nobody blamed them at all.

As we left the Stadio delle Alpi stadium and got on our coach, we noticed the German team on the bus next to us. They looked even more miserable than we did! They were sipping on water and looked shattered. Meanwhile, a crate of beer quickly emerged on our bus, and before we knew it we were all singing, "Doe, a deer, a female deer..." – that song from *The Sound of Music*. For some reason, it often got sung on journeys during Italia '90 – it was just a daft thing, but it lightened the mood and our tears slowly turned to smiles.

Despite the way it all ended, I'll always look back at the World Cup of 1990 as being one of the most joyful periods of my life. It wasn't just the football, it was the feeling of being young, in a foreign country, and having a laugh with all my mates. I'd had a blast, and although I didn't realise it at the time, my life had just changed forever.

4

GAZZAMANIA

ON THE PLANE BACK TO ENGLAND AFTER THE
1990 World Cup, Gary Lineker turned to me and said: "Are
you prepared?"

"For what?" I asked him.

"Life's about to change," he replied.

I didn't really understand what he meant at the time, although
I knew he'd been the hero of the 1986 World Cup, scoring six
goals and winning the Golden Boot, and had received loads of
attention when he came back to England. But we hadn't won
the tournament, we hadn't even made it to the final, so I wasn't
expecting much of a welcome when we landed at Luton.

Big mistake. We arrived to a crowd of about 300,000 fans, all
shouting: "Gazza! Gazza! Gazza!"

It was absolute chaos and at some point a guy handed me a
pair of fake plastic breasts and a belly and, wanting to oblige, I
put the costume on, while the press photographers had a field

day. The joke was on me – I was a fat bastard, with a flabby stomach and man boobs, but I didn't care, it was a laugh and I was happy to play along.

We jumped on a parade bus, and all through the streets of Luton, the fans cheered and saluted us – it was a homecoming like no other.

I'd been in Italy, so I hadn't known that the footage of me crying had been replayed over and over again in England, and that I'd captured the hearts of the nation, as the footballer who felt so deeply about the game. Everywhere I went, the public couldn't get enough of me and I was mobbed and given free champagne in all the bars while the money rolled in. Mel and Len were overwhelmed by requests, and ended up turning most of them down. I was asked to endorse all sorts, including lunch boxes, rugs, T-shirts and key-rings.

I was opening shops for as much as £15k, just to be there for 20 minutes, and I was also doing loads of adverts, including for McDonald's, Walkers Crisps and Adidas. But there was a common theme – no matter what the advert, the producers wanted me crying my eyes out.

I didn't mind, as all this paid very well, and there was so much interest in me, my mam and Anna set up a fan club called Paul Gascoigne Promotions. It sold merchandise such as Gazza badges, and dealt with the huge quantity of fan mail I received every single day.

Girls would send used knickers in the post and it got too much for my mam after a while. A fella sent a letter to me, which she'd opened and read. He'd written: "I know where you live. I am going to handcuff you to the bed, and fuck you all over the place."

My mam rang me up and said: "Son, I can't do this anymore."

The number of letters they had to deal with was insane – there were constantly two to three black bin bags full of mail next to the desk, waiting to be sorted. I tried to persuade my mam to stay. "You've done a brilliant job," I told her. "Please come back!"

But she refused, she'd had enough, and who can blame her?

I was being given freebies all the time and I didn't have to put my hand in my pocket for anything, even though I had plenty of cash. All these years later people still do me favours and give me stuff for free, just because of who I am. Only the other day, I was in Costa Coffee when I pulled out my wallet and realised all my cards were missing.

"Sorry mate," I told the barista. "I'd forgotten that I've lost all my cards, I don't have any cash on me. Can I come back tomorrow?"

"Don't worry about it," he told me, smiling and handing me the coffee for free.

I remember going to Barbados on holiday soon after the World Cup, staring in awe at some huts in Bridgetown, which had my name on them. The people living in them had daubed "Gazza!" and "We love Gazza!" on the walls.

I just thought: "Jesus Christ. I'm on the other side of the world, and everyone knows who I am!"

The downside of my fame was that I got followed by the press pretty much everywhere I went, and I developed a nose for it – I knew when someone was tracking me. I'd be in a taxi, and I'd see a car in the rearview mirror and say to the cabbie: "Pull over here."

I'd then watch as sure enough, the vehicle parked up behind

us. The police in London were actually brilliant when this happened. I'd ring them up, and a cop car would arrive within a few minutes and block the bastards in so I'd be free to leave. It was a mad few years, and my time off the pitch was constantly filled with all kinds of activities.

I famously recorded a version of 'Fog on the Tyne' with Tyneside group Lindisfarne, which got into the top ten and earned me a gold disc, but I got some stick in the dressing room over that.

The thing I was most proud of was being awarded BBC Sports Personality of the Year at a ceremony in Birmingham. I hadn't had anything to drink, and I was sick with nerves as I made my way up to the stage, where Bobby Charlton was standing.

I almost couldn't get my words out, but eventually I managed to say: "I haven't won anything in the game as of yet, but the World Cup did help to put England on the map again."

The truth was, I was really honoured to have been handed that award, and by the legendary Bobby Charlton of all people.

There was so much going on off the pitch that Terry Venables, my manager at Tottenham, imposed a rule which meant I wasn't allowed to do any commercial or non-club related activities for 72 hours before a match. That was fine by me, as it helped to focus my mind on football.

I got slagged off a lot in the press, however, with journalists speculating I was opening too many shops, and it was putting me off my game – but in actual fact I was playing out of my skin, and there was no way cutting a few ribbons was going to change that.

I remember one particular article criticised me heavily, but the very next day I scored a hat-trick against Peter Shilton. Tottenham were playing Derby County at White Hart Lane in September 1990 and I hit the back of the net three times. The second and third goals were the result of free-kicks, and poor Shilton didn't stand a chance.

He was sponsored by mobile phone company Sony Ericsson and, taking the piss, I said to him: "Listen, next time, take your phone with you, keep it by the goal post, and if I get a free-kick I will give you a call and let you know where I am going to put it, so you can save it."

It's true that some women would throw themselves at me in the wake of the World Cup, but in fact it had been happening before the tournament as well. About a week before I went to Italy an absolutely gorgeous blonde girl approached me in London.

"Here, have this," she said, handing me a picture of her wearing a sexy Christmas outfit, with half her boobs on show.

"I'll ring you when I am back from the World Cup and we'll go out," I told her with a wink.

At Luton Airport, waiting for our flight to Italy, I was having a browse of the papers when all of a sudden I spotted a familiar face on the front of a porn magazine.

"That's the girl I spoke to in London!" I exclaimed.

I gave her a ring and said: "You're a fucking porn star."

She replied: "Yeah, I am. I'm in the latest Electric Blue video. Take a watch and you'll love it."

But did I fuck, no way, fat chance of me ever going out with a porn star, my mam would have had a fit!

I'd open a newspaper sometimes, and see a headline which read something like: "My night of passion with Gazza!"

I'd have a read, and the girl would be talking about how amazing I was in bed, and how she gave me ten out of ten.

"I've never met that lass in my life," I'd think to myself, but it was hard to mind when I was being painted in such a positive light.

Much later, after I'd moved to Bournemouth, I was actually stalked by one woman, which was pretty scary. The girl, whoever she was, was persistent, as it was an effort for me to even get into the building, take the lift, and find the flat where I lived at that time. She bombarded me with flowers and letters, professing undying love, and even tracked me down when I had a stint in rehab.

One of the greatest joys of Gazzamania, and the money it brought, was the ability it gave me to shower my family with gifts, the more generous the better. I bought them all sorts over the years including jewelry, designer clothes, bikes for the kids – I even got my dad a boat, a motorhome and God knows how many cars.

I probably got the most joy from giving Lindsay a Ford Escort XR3i convertible when she was still just 19, as a Christmas present. It cost £17k which was a hell of a lot of money back then, and I arranged for the garage to wrap it up in a huge red bow. A few days before Christmas Day I drove Lindsay to the garage to have a look at it.

"That's your Christmas present," I told her, pointing to the white sports car, which had a black leather soft top.

"Oh, wow," she exclaimed. "It's absolutely gorgeous!"

There were also the holidays I was able to pay for, and I'll never forget the trip we all took to Disney World in Florida in 1992. We stayed at the Grand Floridian five star hotel, right on the edge of the park, and it was an amazing experience. It was right next to a manmade lake and a few days before we arrived a 9ft alligator had strolled into the lobby of the hotel. There were signs all over the place saying: "Beware of the alligators."

We were terrified when we took a boat out onto that lake, all of us, screaming and laughing at the same time, but it was tremendous fun. To add to the excitement, the hotel was full of celebrities, including Hulk Hogan, basketball player Michael Jordan and Nancy Cartwright, the voice of Bart Simpson. The funny thing about Nancy was that she actually looked and sounded just like a 14-year-old boy – we all thought that was brilliant. I didn't get quite as much attention in the US as I did in the UK, so I was made up when Michael Jordan recognised me, and said hello.

Lindsay, Carl, Anna and my mam and dad were in their element. We were just a normal family from Dunston, staying in a world class resort, rubbing shoulders with the rich and famous, and we were having the time of our lives. As a matter of fact, in a short amount of time, I'd joined their ranks. I was rich and famous myself, and we were all sharing in the joy that brought.

The astonishing fame I experienced in the wake of the World Cup certainly had its stresses and I often found it impossible to relax but most of all I remember feeling immense joy throughout that exciting period. The whole world was obsessed with me and what's more, I was still a young lad, with so much left to do. I look back now and realise it was a truly glorious time. I felt invincible and was full of such hope for the future.

3 ANTICIPATION

PROLOGUE

ANTICIPATION – An emotion involving pleasure, anxiety or excitement in considering or awaiting an expected event.

"KATIE," I SAY, "I THINK I MIGHT HAVE A DRINK tomorrow." I tell her lightly, casually, as though it's nothing. The way I say it, I could be letting her know I am planning to go fishing or get my hair cut. But my relaxed manner of speaking fools no-one, and fails to disguise the mild panic in my voice. Carnage is around the corner, and we all know it. Quite frankly, I am a fucking nightmare when I drink. I am warning Katie that a bomb is about to go off.

But she doesn't really react. "OK," she says. Katie knows she can't stop me from picking up a drink and she no longer tries – all she can do is prepare herself. This is the calm before the storm.

When I am drinking, it's awful for everyone, but equally,

during my periods of sobriety, a terrible anticipation hangs in the air. Everybody knows it's not a question of IF I will hit the bottle again, but WHEN.

As I've already said, I've accepted now that I will never stop drinking. I am an alcoholic and for that reason I am always anticipating my next drink.

Drinking aside, I am an impatient bastard and I struggle to sit still, or stand in a queue and wait. It drives me crazy, and I get bored so easily, I always have. Strangely, the only thing which calms me down is fishing. Waiting to pay for my fags at the newsagent? Agony. Waiting for a fish? Fucking bliss. For some reason, sitting with a fishing rod in my hand, anticipating the tug of the line, is the only time my mind clears and I am worry-free.

Back when I was playing football, the feeling of anticipation was the same, but the circumstances were very different. The excitement, the nerves, the stress of waiting for important games to come around, was intoxicating. Sometimes I dealt with it well, other times not so good.

I guess everyone will remember the 1991 FA Cup final, and how fired up I was at the start of that game against Nottingham Forest. It didn't end well for me on that occasion, to say the least. But there were also times when my passion, my fierce determination to get out there and take a game by the scruff of the neck, paid off handsomely.

As a general rule, swigging brandy before a match is not to be recommended – but I did it on many occasions. It was my secret weapon. I loved the sensation of it hitting the back of my throat, then warming my empty stomach. It took the edge off my nerves, but also stoked the fire in my belly.

Mostly, I simply couldn't wait to shut the critics up, to ram their words back down their throats, and the only way to do that was to play brilliant football. As in Euro '96, for instance, when a lot of people wanted me thrown out of the England squad – even some members of the Football Association – due to my admittedly questionable behaviour off the pitch. The only way to fight back was to absolutely smash it and I did. I scored a spectacular goal against Scotland, leading to a 2-0 win for England, just days after I was hammered in the papers over my drunken antics in Hong Kong.

Then, there was the time I waited a whole year before making my debut for Lazio – 12 months out of action, with fans in Italy desperate for me to start playing for their team. That was a year of rehabilitation, recovery, disappointment and anxiety over whether I would ever play football again. But in the main, I feel I handled the stress and nerves created by anticipation as best as I could and really, when it comes down to it, I have no regrets about how it all played out. None at all.

1

FA CUP FINAL '91

IN BLAZING SUNSHINE, I WATCHED SPELLBOUND as the teams walked onto the pitch in their brand new suits, ahead of the biggest match of the year. This is what I loved best as a kid, the build up to the FA Cup final, the anticipation of it, and then the game itself, always played out beneath bright blue skies. Maybe I'm looking back with rose tinted spectacles, but every cup final match seemed to take place on a lovely, sunny day and nothing came close to the excitement of those games.

It was never my dream to win a World Cup, or a European Championship. As a bairn, all I ever wanted was to lift the FA Cup at Wembley, to walk up those 39 steps and hoist aloft that famous trophy. But little did I know that when I did finally get to play in an FA Cup final, it would turn out to be a nightmare, ending after just 17 minutes and putting me out of action for a whole year.

To begin with, I reckon I was playing some of the best football of my career during that 1991 FA Cup run. As we breezed past Blackpool, Oxford United, Portsmouth and Notts County, I felt invincible. We easily made it to the FA Cup semi-final to face our North London rivals, Arsenal. It was the first time a semi-final, usually held in Sheffield, Manchester or Birmingham, had ever been played at Wembley, so both sets of supporters were able to attend the match without having to travel. Arsenal at that time were the best team in the country, and were going for the league and cup double – they were red-hot favourites to win. I was massively fired up for the game, having battled back from a double hernia operation in the nick of time.

But it's funny how things work out.

After five minutes, I scored from a 30-yard free-kick – it was one of the best goals of my career, and it inspired us to a 3-1 victory. That goal settled me right down and I was able to stay level-headed and calm enough to help the team defeat our bitter rivals. Had the same thing happened in the final itself, who knows how different things may have been?

I was elated to reach the FA Cup final, we all were, and the anticipation ahead of that big game was like nothing else. We all went to get measured for our brand new suits and the mood among the lads was electrifying.

However, there was the small problem of Tottenham's finances rumbling away in the background, and casting a shadow over what was otherwise an exciting time for the team. The club was struggling, and had already sold Chris Waddle to Marseille for £4.25million a few years earlier, in 1989, to make a quick buck. Now, they'd set their sights on me. I discovered Spurs were having talks with Italian club Lazio, and it really pissed me off that it was all happening without my involvement or knowledge. I felt like a commodity they wanted to cash in on. Despite this, Mel and Len travelled to Italy to start negotiations with Lazio's general manager Maurizio Manzini, and a fee of £8.5million was agreed. I hadn't wanted to leave, I was really happy at Tottenham, but the club was desperate for money – debts of £10million had been rumoured – and I was the obvious player to sell. I was annoyed, but the truth was, I was also excited by the prospect of a new life abroad. It was a chance to leave all the bad press behind and start over again.

But I am afraid the negotiations tainted the FA Cup final, where we were to play Brian Clough's young Nottingham Forest side, as I realised this was going to be my final game for Tottenham. I had recovered enough from my hernia to be fit to play, and everything pointed towards a fairytale ending to my time at the club.

Unfortunately, I'd whipped myself into a real frenzy ahead of the game. I was just so excited, I couldn't help it. I'd bought dozens of tickets for all my family and friends, which probably didn't help. Every bugger I knew was sitting in that stadium and I was desperate to perform for them.

But I'll admit, it was quite normal for me to go out onto the pitch in a revved-up state, just like I had in the semi-final against Arsenal and on many more occasions. It's how I was and how I got the best out of myself. Within the first minute, I had kicked Forest's Garry Parker in the chest after following through with a high challenge. The referee, Roger Milford, could easily have sent me off there and then, but he could see it had been a reckless, rather than malicious, challenge, and I was spared.

Ten minutes later, with the score still 0-0 I had somehow got myself into the centre-half position, and their left-back Gary

Charles was heading straight for me, powering dangerously towards the goal. I instinctively lunged at him and brought him crashing to the ground. It was an awful challenge, I admit, and it left me writhing on the floor in agony. The ironic thing was, just a few days earlier, I had taken part in a video tutorial instructing young kids to avoid exactly that type of move.

"Always make sure your body is behind the ball to protect yourself from injury when making a block tackle," I told them. What an idiot I'd been. Why hadn't I taken my own advice?

Somehow I managed to get back on my feet and stand in the wall for the Forest free-kick I'd conceded, looking on as Stuart Pearce smashed the ball into the net to put Nottingham Forest 1-0 ahead. But my mind was elsewhere – I was in so much pain that I crumpled to the floor. I'd lasted just 17 minutes of the FA Cup final, and now I was being stretchered off the pitch in total agony.

I reached the dressing room in bits, with just one question on my lips. "How long will it take for me to recover? A couple of weeks?" I asked our physio John Sheridan.

"No," he replied, shaking his head.

"A few months?" I said, panic building within me.

"I'm sorry, Gazza," he told me. "It will take you at least nine months to recover from a cruciate ligament injury." Well, I broke down upon hearing that. The ambulance arrived to take me to the Princess Grace Hospital, and they had the radio on so I could listen to the commentary from Wembley. I heard the roar of the crowd when Paul Stewart equalised for us, and I was able to watch extra-time on TV in the hospital to see Forest's Des Walker score an own goal to win us the cup, 2-1.

"Can I go to the victory party?" I asked the doctor.

"No chance, sorry," he told me and I was gutted. There was nothing else for it – I swallowed my disappointment and settled into my hospital bed.

But before I knew what was happening, the entire team had burst into my room, juggling the FA Cup between them. I felt a right idiot, lying there, the dozy sod who'd almost cost them the win, but it was an amazing gesture.

I later learnt that manager Terry Venables had gathered all the players together in the dressing room after the game and said: "Right, we're going to see Gazza in hospital. Let's go!"

I managed to hold it together while the lads were in the room, but once they left I couldn't stop crying. My Tottenham career had ended in the most heartbreaking way – an FA Cup winner, but crocked in a hospital bed with no prospect of playing football again for almost a whole year.

My mam and dad had been at Wembley, and had watched the whole sorry debacle play out, so they came to the hospital to see me.

It was good to have them there, but I didn't want my parents hanging around. I was upset and worried, and I was eager to be on my own. I didn't want them to see me like that.

"Get yourselves back to Gateshead," I told them. "I'll be alreet."

"Son, we're at least staying until they take you for your op," my mam said.

When I finally woke up, I looked groggily around the room, and was pleased to discover I was alone – but then my eyes fell upon my bedside table. Before I'd gone in for my op, my FA Cup winners medal had been there along with a solid gold watch presented to me by Lazio – it must have been worth an absolute fortune.

"Nurse, I've been robbed!" I exclaimed.

"Don't worry," she told me. "Your mum's taken the medal, and your dad has the watch."

"Fucking great!" I thought to myself. I knew I'd never see the watch or the medal again. I was pissed off, but that was my mam and dad for you. They probably thought they were doing me a favour and the truth was I would have given them my last tenner if it had come down to it. I didn't begrudge them a thing.

As I lay there in hospital, I reflected on my time at Tottenham. Most of all, I felt incredibly lucky to have played for the club, and later England, under Terry Venables. He was a fantastic coach and manager, full of ideas on the training pitch and a calm, reassuring presence whenever I had a problem. He was always very fair to the players, and normally resolved issues in an adult way without too much nastiness. It turned out Chris Waddle and Glenn Roeder had been bang on when they'd told me I was going to love working with him.

The man had looked after me and really helped to develop my game. I owed him the world, but it didn't stop me from crossing the line once or twice.

I remember on one occasion, we had been defeated in a horrible match. It had been pissing it down, and afterwards, I was venting at everyone in the dressing room. I couldn't help it, I was furious.

"You soft southern shites!" I told them. "Afraid of the rain and the cold?" I spat.

Venners had a bit of a go at me, advised me to calm down, but instead of apologising, I retorted: "You can fuck off, and all." Not a clever thing to do.

Very quietly, as unusually for a manager, the gaffer was a man who rarely swore and hardly ever raised his voice, he said: "Come and see me in my office."

I was absolutely shitting myself, but as I made my way there, I had an idea.

"I know," I thought to myself, "I'll get him a drink."

I stopped off at the players' lounge and picked up two pints of lager.

When I got to his office I handed him one of the pints as a peace offering.

"I am so sorry," I told him, "I promise never to do that ever again."

"I could fine you," he said, but I noticed he had a slight smile on his face.

Then, he added: "I probably should fine you for bringing me beer instead of wine! Don't let it happen again!"

I think Terry probably found it harder to forgive me when I upset his dad, Fred. His father ran a pub, The Royal Oak, close to the hotel I was living in at the time, so one day I decided to go and see him and say hello. While there, I heard a noise outside.

"What's that?" I asked Fred.

"It's my pet pheasant," he replied.

"Ah, I love shooting pheasants," I told him.

But Fred warned me off, saying: "Leave that bird alone. I've had him for years." I promised not to touch it, and went on my way. But all night, I couldn't stop thinking about what a laugh it would be to go back on my word.

The next morning, I picked up my rifle, went over to the pub, popped the pheasant and carried it back to the hotel in my gun bag. Why did I have a gun bag? I've always been into hunting, so I often kept guns safely with me.

"Here," I told the kitchen staff. "Cook this for me, will you?"

The next day, Terry called me into his office. "Where's my dad's fucking pheasant?" he asked. I could only grin and rub my belly in reply.

During our first season together, in 1988/89, I scored seven goals, made 37 appearances and we finished sixth in the league. The following season, 1989/90, we finished third. Gary Lineker had joined us by then, and we developed a fantastic relationship on the pitch. When Gary first arrived, he struggled to get off the mark – it took him about six games before he scored his first goal. "I thought you said he was a goal machine?" I joked with the gaffer, knowing full well the goals would start flowing soon enough – and once he got his first, there was no stopping him. He got a hat-trick in his next game and ended up scoring 26 goals that season. I got seven again that year, playing 38 times.

Gary was famous for never receiving a yellow card in his whole career – he claimed he just didn't have a temper – but I remember making him angry once or twice! Especially when I'd drive to his house in St John's Wood, a really posh area of London, and leave my car on his front drive while I went into the city – blocking his own vehicle in. He would be spitting feathers by the time I saw him next.

It was just a shame that Chris Waddle was sold before that season started, as the club needed the £4.25million Marseille were prepared to pay for him. He'd been our star player during the 1988/89 season and he blossomed in France, where he was able to display his skills without having to worry about defending. There had been talk of us signing Peter Beardsley when Gary joined – can you imagine a line-up of Gazza, Waddle, Beardsley and Lineker? What a team that would have been!

Our dressing room was a potent mix of flash bastards, crackpots, hard men and dedicated professionals. You would never find better examples of how to behave as a footballer than Gary Lineker and our captain Gary Mabbutt – they were flawless, and everyone had so much respect for them both. Whereas myself and John Moncur were totally daft, as was Steve Sedgley. I remember Steve once directing the traffic from a roundabout while stark bollock naked, pretending to be a road policeman. And I almost got John into big trouble the night before our FA Cup fifth round tie against Portsmouth in February 1991.

I couldn't sleep, so I woke up John and pestered him to have a game of squash with me in the hotel.

"Just one game, please?" I begged.

He agreed, but one game turned into 11, and two hours later we were both knackered. The next day, on the coach to the game I could barely move, I was so sore – not great preparation for such an important match. John was alright, as he was only a substitute – but the team were relying on me to get us through to the quarter-finals and for the first half of the game, I was awful. It was no surprise we ended up 1-0 behind at half time. Somehow, I managed to improve my game and scored two goals to get us into the next round. Of course, the gaffer later heard all about the squash incident and launched an investigation to find out which players were involved. He probably guessed it was me right away, and he didn't really bollock me that much. But John never got caught, luckily for him.

It took me a year to recover from my cruciate ligament injury. The surgeon John Browett worked wonders in repairing my shattered right knee, and the Spurs physio John Sheridan was there to help with every stage of my rehabilitation.

In June 1991, we took a trip to Portugal to help me convalesce with lots of swimming and intense exercise regimes. My dad, Jimmy and John-Paul, my sister Anna's husband, came along too, and we had some laughs amongst the hard work, even going shark fishing on one occasion.

I spent hour upon hour on the exercise bike and clambering up steps at Tottenham's Hog Hill training ground car park, coming in early in the morning to avoid seeing all the lads training on the pitch. I was making good progress when, in July 1991, my sister Lindsay was punched in the stomach outside Ristorante Roma in Newcastle and knocked to the ground. I retaliated and accidentally lashed out at the wrong person, which of course made me seem like the aggressor in all the news stories. At least the Italian press portrayed me as a hero, coming to the rescue of my teenage sister.

I guess that should have been a warning, but worse was to follow in September when, during another trip to Newcastle, I was attacked in a club called Walkers. I'd been to watch Newcastle take on Derby County earlier in the day, then enjoyed a trip to my beloved Dunston Excelsior, before heading into town with some mates.

We had only been in the bar for around an hour, and I'd just returned from the toilets with my brother when some jealous bastard shouted: "Gazza!" The next thing I knew I'd been smacked on the chin and was on the ground. I felt my kneecap give way, and could tell instantly that all the hard work I'd put in since the operation had been ruined in a split second.

It had all been going so well. By August, I had started jogging for the first time, the support wires had been removed from my kneecap, I was cycling around the training ground, and I had also been unveiled to the Lazio supporters in front of a frenzied crowd in Rome. There were banners and flags welcoming me to the team, even though I hadn't officially signed yet, and I was excited to be joining such a passionate club. The crowd were singing "Paul Gascoigne, la la la" while I read a short message on the pitch. I met the coach, former Italy goalkeeper Dino Zoff, who had captained his country to World Cup glory in 1982, and the club expressed their wish for me to join as soon as possible. Hence the reason for my visit to the North East the following month, so I could say goodbye to my mates in Dunston before starting a new life in Italy.

The attack set my recovery back by a number of months, and I required a further operation at the Princess Grace Hospital, but I wasn't going to let the actions of one moron get me down – it made me even more determined to come back better than ever. By Christmas, I was back jogging again, and by February 1992, I was taking part in light training sessions. John Sheridan and I made a second trip to Lazio at the end of that month so they could monitor my progress, and by the end of April I was able to play in my first behind closed doors football match. Almost 12 months had passed since the 1991 FA Cup final, but at last – I was back!

2

LAZIO

I FINALLY SIGNED FOR LAZIO IN MAY 1992, FOR
the fee of £5.5 million. After getting involved in the negotiations
myself, I was made up with the £2 million signing-on fee, which
I immediately splashed on my family, paying for that epic trip
to Disney World in Florida for my mam, dad, brother, sisters
and their partners, as well as Jimmy and my partner Sheryl. I
also bought them all houses, cars and luxury holidays. Lazio
looked after their players very well, employing bodyguards for
each of us, and my two guards – Johnny and Augusto – kept me
company when I moved into my villa in Rome.

On my first day of training with my new teammates, I brought
with me 20 copies of *Teach Yourself English* and left them on the
benches for the other players. Hey, did they think I was going
to learn Italian? Actually, I did make an effort to learn some of
the language, but only the swear words.

The club sent two Italian girls to my hotel to help me out,

which was good of them. I bought them a beer each and said: "Right, you want to teach me Italian? Great, I'll write down the words I'd like to know."

Putting pen to paper, I wrote "fanny", "want a fuck?", "arsehole", "fuck right off" and "get to fuck".

"That's all I need to know," I told them.

It was very childish, I'll admit that now, and looking back it's not surprising they didn't seem amused. The lasses promptly left, and they never came back. I didn't mean to be disrespectful, but I had tunnel vision. It was football I was interested in, nothing else.

Dutch player Aron Winter signed for Lazio at roughly the same time, and we found ourselves sharing a hotel, so I decided to go and introduce myself to him properly – but I wanted to make an impression.

I stripped off all my clothes and knocked on his door, stark bollock naked, but to my horror it was his wife who appeared on the threshold. I could see Winter in the background and quickly said: "Hiya, pleased to meet you, mate. See you tomorrow, in training."

By this point, the players were probably wondering who the hell I thought I was, and the bosses were quite possibly questioning their decision to sign me.

Nevertheless, I made my debut against Genoa on September 27th. The game was broadcast live in the UK, as were most of my appearances for Lazio during that first year, as Channel 4 had bought the rights to show Serie A matches in their new *Football Italia* programme.

A few weeks into the new season, we got thumped 5-3 by AC Milan at the San Siro. They were an amazing side, with the likes of Franco Baresi, Paolo Maldini, Marco van Basten and Frank Rijkaard on their team, but I still felt embarrassed by our display and I didn't hold back in the dressing room afterwards. But they were a great bunch of lads, and we very rarely had any fights or rows during my time there. I was still able to play the odd prank now and again, too.

I found a two-foot long snake in my bedroom one morning, so I stunned it with a broom and put it in a bag. Later that day, at training while the lads were out, I put the dazed reptile in Roberto Di Matteo's coat pocket. He came in afterwards and I said to him: "I've left my wallet at home – do you have any spare cash on you?" He replied that he did, and went to reach into his pocket. I've never seen anyone jump so high in all my life – he properly shat himself. But he took it in good humour eventually, as well as can be expected anyway.

It wasn't the only time I surprised the other players with an animal. I took a mouse with me to the Lazio-Roma derby, don't ask me why. I suppose joking around was my way of relaxing. There were 105,000 fans in the stadium and I knew the other players would be shitting themselves. So, to lighten the mood, I bought a little mouse from a pet shop, and put it in the top pocket of my jacket. During the team talk I just stood there, with this tiny creature pushing its head out of my pocket, while the lads did their very best to keep straight faces. We went out, played some brilliant football, then when we came back, I spotted the mouse in the corner of the dressing room. I quickly picked it up, put it back in my pocket, then fucked off.

I had my fair share of run-ins with the Italian media, who were often even bigger arseholes than the English press. I punched one reporter in the bollocks for all the crap he had been writing about me, and I also whacked one overly persistent photographer, having warned him to keep away from my family. The paparazzi were a disgrace, taking photos of Sheryl's children Mason and Bianca until it reached the stage the kids didn't want to go out anymore – stuff like that broke your heart.

My relationship with the fans had been fantastic since the very beginning, but our love affair was cemented in November when I got a late equaliser against our fierce rivals Roma to earn us a 1-1 draw. What a time to score your first goal for your new club! I had never experienced such emotion before, and the relief was incredible.

Having said that, in Italy, if you had a bad game, which was rare for me, the fans would kick your car. When I found out, it finally made sense why all the players drove bangers, despite having millions in the bank. After one particular match, I got back to the car park, to find one guy having a real go at my vehicle. "I'm not standing for that," I thought. I jumped into my car as quickly as I could, reversed over him, picked him up, then bundled him onto the back seat. I then went to get the club physio and told him: "Sort that bastard out. He won't be doing that again." And I was right, the bloke wasn't seriously injured, but none of the fans touched my car from then on.

The Lazio supporters loved and respected me, that much was obvious, but I didn't have the same close relationship with the club's hierarchy.

In January 1993, I'd been left out of a game against Juventus and afterwards I was walking past a group of reporters with the owner's son, Andrea Cragnotti. A reporter stuck a microphone in front of my face and asked me how I felt. The media at that point were really getting on my nerves, and so instead of saying something, I let out a loud burp. Unbeknownst to me, that belch was filmed by live TV, and broadcast to millions of Italians, just as they were sitting down for their evening meal. If the same thing had happened in England, I think the press would have found it amusing, but in Italy, there were calls for me to be thrown out of the country – people were outraged. The incident was even mentioned in the Italian Parliament.

Lazio's owner, Sergio Cragnotti, was especially upset. I'd already annoyed him when I first joined the club by saying to him, "Tua figlia, grande tette", roughly translated as, "Your daughter, big tits." I had been wearing a club blazer at the time of the burp, and so in his mind I had brought shame on Lazio's good name. But the fans saw the funny side, singing "Gazza, Gazza, give us a belch" during the next match.

I fell out with the club on another occasion when they tried to make me play in a charity match against Diego Maradona's Sevilla. I was pissed off as the friendly clashed with a game against Juventus, which I really wanted to play in. "Fuck this," I thought, and I decided to fly off to EuroDisney in Paris instead. There were frantic calls from Lazio, begging me to return, and I only relented when they promised to pay me £120,000 in appearance money. So I went back, played while half drunk after guzzling champagne on the flight, and beat at least three players to score a goal, with the match ending 1-1. "I'm a bit pissed," I told Diego in the tunnel before the game. "Don't worry, Gazza," he replied. "So am I."

Lazio didn't pay me £120,000 in the end, instead they docked £40,000 from my wages, so I fucked off back to EuroDisney, where I felt more at home.

But on the whole, my first season at Lazio went well, and I

managed to stay relatively injury free until April 1993, when I broke my cheekbone in an England match against Holland. After that, I was forced to wear a *Phantom of the Opera* style face mask for the rest of the season, to protect the injury. Lazio finished in fifth place in Serie A, qualifying for Europe for the first time since the 1970s.

My second season in Italy was blighted by weight issues, and I was ordered to lose two stone by the end of pre season training or else I wouldn't be in the team. I managed to do this by consuming only water and lemon, with the occasional chicken sandwich every now and then, and lots of running in bin liners.

One day during training, I got pulled aside by coach Dino Zoff, who said someone extremely important was on the phone.

"Who is it?" I asked.

"The Pope," he said.

"Fucking hell," I thought, "No-one's more important than The Pope."

I went into Zoff's office and picked up the phone. "Alreet, Pope?" I asked.

I don't think Pope John Paul II had a clue what I was saying, but he made it clear he wanted to meet me and I was completely honoured. As a lad, he'd been a goalkeeper in his home country of Poland, and he had met Jack Charlton's Ireland team during Italia '90, so I guess he was a big football fan. I missed seeing him by five minutes, as training overran, but at least my mam, dad and sister Anna, who were staying with me at the time, got to meet him and were given little gifts. When I finally arrived at the Vatican his cardinal presented me with a big gold medal – I immediately called Jimmy and asked him to fly over to collect it, and take it home for safekeeping.

My second season came to a premature end in April 1994, when I suffered a broken leg during training. I had recently captained the side and things were going well. Terry Venables had just been made England manager too, so it happened at a particularly bad time. It ruled me out for most of the following season, by which point Dino Zoff had been replaced by Zdenek Zeman, a tough taskmaster who ran us into the ground. It soon became clear that I didn't figure in his plans, so by the summer of 1995 I knew my Italian adventure would be coming to an end.

I loved my time in Italy. I loved the double training sessions, the Italian culture, the food, the football, the weather, the fans … I was really sad to be leaving it all behind, but at the same time just as excited for what the future held at my new club, Glasgow Rangers.

3

RANGERS

TOWARDS THE END OF MY TIME AT LAZIO, I WAS
feeling miserable. I'd had my share of injuries – broken legs,
fractured cheekbones – and I wanted to get away, so I asked
what teams were interested in me. The Italians mentioned
Glasgow Rangers, which immediately caught my attention. I'd
followed them over the years and understood what a massive
club they were, but what clinched the move was their manager
Walter Smith coming over to see me.

I'd actually first met Walter a few summers earlier while on
holiday in Florida. Sheryl and I were sunbathing on the beach
and I spotted him carrying a big ice bucket with his sons by his
side. "He's got some beers in there," I thought to myself, and I
turned to Sheryl and said: "That's Walter Smith, the manager
of Glasgow Rangers. God, I'd love to play for them." I then
spent the rest of the afternoon playing American Football with
his young son, deliberately throwing the ball above his head so

it would land on the sunbathers behind him. Then, when the poor lad went to retrieve the ball he'd get a load of abuse from the person it had hit.

So I was delighted when, a couple of years later, Walter set his sights on me, and came out to Italy to try and persuade me to join Rangers. I saw Walter approaching the gates of my villa while I was sitting by the pool with Jimmy, and he seemed a bit nervous, but he came over and said: "Let me tell you about the club." I just looked at him and said: "Jimmy, get two beers. Walter, I'm signing."

I then spoke to the chairman, Sir David Murray, who said: "I've got your house sorted already." And that was it, I left without even packing a suitcase – I just got on a flight, I couldn't wait.

"You seem a bit sad," Walter had told me. "Come to our club and we'll put a smile back on your face. You'll love it and you will start enjoying your football again."

That was all I needed to hear, and Walter was right – I had the best time playing for Rangers – we won a shedload of trophies, we had the most incredible supporters, and my teammates – Ally McCoist, Ian Durrant, Gordon Durie, Stuart McCall, Andy Goram, Richard Gough – were a great bunch of lads.

I signed in July 1995 for £4.3million, the most expensive signing in the club's history, just as when I'd signed for Spurs in 1988 and Lazio in 1992. To be a bit different, I bleached my hair when I joined and I also got my top set of teeth fixed. I had them capped to hide how horrendous they had become. Ally McCoist found it hilarious – "You could eat an apple through a letterbox," he laughed.

Our squad was top quality. I used to give Terry Butcher grief when he played for Rangers in the late 80s, saying the Scottish Division wasn't a proper league, and he'd reply: "Don't mock it until you try it." When I first arrived I probably thought it would be easier compared to the English and Italian leagues, but it wasn't at all. We used to play a practice game in every training session, and they were like cup finals, as everyone was desperate to get into the side – a squad of 16 full internationals fighting like mad for a place in the first XI on Saturday.

I also had some extra motivation when I joined, as the Scottish press kept saying I wouldn't do well up there. Who were they kidding? I could have played blindfolded half the time! I remember playing against a cocky young kid who said he was going to get the better of me. Well, I scored two against him, we won 2-1, and after the game I went into his dressing room, took my boots off and gave them to him. "One day you might fucking play like that," I told him, and walked out.

I must admit to doing a few stupid things when I first joined, such as pretending to play the flute after I'd scored in a pre-season friendly against Steaua Bucharest. But I was only doing what my teammates had told me, they said it would go down a storm with the Rangers fans, so stupidly, I did it. I had no idea it was a way of mocking Catholic Celtic supporters, mimicking flute players marching in the Orange parade.

The standard in Scotland was mixed – you had tremendous sides like Celtic and Aberdeen, where you always had to be at your best to come away with a result. But often the teams we faced were poor, and this hampered our progress in Europe. Imagine, one minute you're playing against Kilmarnock and Partick Thistle, and then the next game you're facing Ajax in the Champions League. The difference in quality made it so much more difficult for us to adjust our game, and I think that's why we struggled so much in the big European games.

But, other than that, my first season at Rangers was one of the highlights of my career, and it ended with me scoring a hat-trick against Aberdeen to win the club's eighth consecutive Scottish Premier Division title. Aside from the FA Cup win in 1991, where I'd only lasted 17 minutes, this was the first trophy of my career, and to score a hat-trick in the decisive game was an unbelievable feeling.

We had also reached the Scottish Cup final. Assistant Archie Knox would urge us on, saying: "Come on lads, I can smell hot dogs" – meaning we were almost at Hampden Park. God, I loved it when he said that – it summed up the spirit and camaraderie within the group, that we were on the verge of achieving special things. Three weeks after we won the league, we then beat Hearts in the Scottish Cup final to clinch the Double. And, as the season drew to a close, I started to collect all the big awards. I won the Player's Player of the Year award as well as the Sportswriters Player of the Year award – I cleaned up that first year.

Drinking did play a part in that success, too. I got into the habit of having a swig of brandy 15 minutes before the start of a match. I'd grab my hip flask, gulp it down, and then put it to one side. None of the staff said anything, as they could see it wasn't harming my performances.

We played Hearts in the Scottish League Cup final in November 1996, and I didn't have the best first half. I had made myself too nervous, with it being a cup final, and was rowing with Ally McCoist when we went into the dressing room at half-time. We were winning 2-1 at the time but I was raging with Coisty so I didn't listen to the manager when he told me to keep quiet. The next thing I know Walter Smith had me pinned to the wall. I quietened down then. Archie Knox then asked me: "Have you had a brandy?"

"No, I haven't," I replied.

"Well, fucking go and get one!" he said.

I apologised to Coisty, then walked into the director's box at Parkhead, where the final was taking place, still wearing my kit and sweating profusely, and asked the barman for a triple brandy. I downed it in front of all the guests, went back to the dressing room, and said: "Thanks Archie."

"Get out there," he said, "and fucking do the business." I then scored two cracking goals to win us the cup, with the match ending 4-3. The lads didn't come too close to me when I was celebrating, mind. I guess the alcohol fumes must have been too much for them.

We had a lot of fun during training, with so many great characters in the dressing room. I remember coming in one morning wearing a pair of waders up to my chest, with a collar and tie and two giant trout in my hands. The lads were falling on the floor laughing, but I was wearing my shirt and tie so Walter couldn't reprimand me. The boys went out to train but Coisty and I were injured so we stayed in the dressing room. "Come on Coisty," I said, "Let's hide the fish in one of the boys' cars." Coisty was well up for it, so we chose Gordon Durie to be our victim.

Coisty grabbed the keys to Durie's Honda, we opened the boot and unscrewed the compartment for the spare tyre, and carefully placed one of the trout inside. Coisty went to hand me the second fish, thinking I'd put the pair of them in the same place. "No, I have a better idea," I told him. So I opened the back door of the Honda, found a secret compartment Coisty never even knew existed, and put the second trout in there. Coisty was baffled, asking me: "Why did you do that?" I tapped my nose and said: "When he finds the first fish, he'll think that's it."

A few days later, Durie came into the dressing room complaining, saying: "The smell in my car is horrendous! It's unbelievable. When I stop at traffic lights, people look away in disgust!" Eventually, he found the fish in the boot. "You're bang out of order," he said. "I know you're responsible, Gazza." Another week went by, and he still couldn't understand why his car smelled so bad. "I just cannae get rid of the stench!" All the boys went to take a look, and we saw his car was filled with air fresheners – those magic tree ones, all colours and sizes, there must have been about 12 of them hanging up everywhere. In the end, his car smelled so bad he had no choice but to send it away to be valeted – and they finally found the second fish. He had to get rid of that car. I don't think the gaffer was too impressed about that.

With Sheryl and I getting married and our son Regan entering our lives, we bought a lovely house in Renfrewshire, not far from where Ally McCoist lived. Well, it was 1.8 miles away from his place, to be exact. I know that because he measured the distance.

There was a pub nearby that I used to visit quite often, and one night feeling quite pissed I suddenly became hungry. It was 2am and everywhere else was closed, so I thought – why not break into Coisty's house? I knew he always left a key under his mat and had a well-stocked kitchen. I snuck in and prepared myself a ginormous sandwich, using all the tins in his cupboards and all the food in his fridge. I must have made a noise, as it woke him up and I could hear him edging his way downstairs, rattling a baseball bat against the banister to scare away the intruder in his home. By this point, I'd tidied up all the mess I'd made and was carefully arranging all the tins on his shelves. "Fucking hell – it's you, Gazza!" he shouted. "I'm going back to bed." So I finished tidying up his kitchen, and then walked back home to my place.

Also around that time, at the end of the 1995/96 season, there was the little matter of Euro '96 to look forward to. England and Scotland had been drawn in the same group, along with Holland and Switzerland, so the abuse I got from the Scottish lads in the run up to the tournament was horrendous. I just kept saying to them: "Look, you've seen how I play for Rangers, but just wait until you see me play for England."

4

EURO '96

I WAS ELATED TO LINK UP WITH TERRY Venables again when he became England manager in January 1994. The previous England boss, Graham Taylor, had been a disaster, so it was no surprise when the FA fired him once England failed to reach the 1994 World Cup. I couldn't wait to start working with Terry again, and I knew that with him in charge, we stood a great chance of winning Euro '96. Furthermore, as the host nation, all our games would be played at Wembley.

I'd previously sought the advice of Chris Waddle and Glenn Roeder when I joined Spurs, and they had all sung Terry's praises. Now, I was the one being asked about him by all the other England players, like Ian Wright and Paul Ince, who had never worked with him before. "He's fucking marvellous," I told them.

The atmosphere in the camp was excellent when compared

to the previous regime, with a new energy and vibrancy among the squad. I played in Terry's first match as England manager, against Denmark at Wembley in March 1994. My hero Bryan Robson was helping Terry as assistant, my mate Peter Beardsley was back and our tactics were better. It felt like the dawn of an exciting new era as we overcame the Danes with an impressive 1-0 victory.

But I had to wait another 15 months before my next game under Terry, as I broke my leg in April '94 while training with Lazio. By the time I next linked up with the England squad, the side was well underway in their preparations for Euro '96. I made an appearance as a substitute against Japan in June 1995, and thankfully from that point onwards I became a fixture in the team again.

At one point Terry even considered making me the captain of the England team. I was playing out of my skin for Rangers, scoring goals and keeping fit, and it would have been an incredible honour to have represented my country in that way. But I knew deep down that the press would have slaughtered me, they would have dredged up all my past indiscretions, and it wouldn't have been fair on the team or myself to place so much negative publicity on the squad. I was more than happy just being part of the first XI.

The anticipation I felt going into Euro '96 was incredible. I had loved Italia '90, being with all the lads, training every day and really enjoying my football, so I couldn't wait to experience it all again as an older and wiser player. But the World Cup '90 had been marred by our relationship with the English press – they had hammered us every single day, the papers filled with scurrilous lies and untrue scandals. They even tried to claim three of our players had slept with a hostess – total bollocks. In the end, we placed a blanket ban on speaking to the written press, and when Paul Parker tried to break it I threw a cup of water over him. Six years on, and the press were still on our backs. They couldn't wait to latch onto anything remotely negative so they could sell their papers with sensational headlines.

In the run up to Euro '96 we went on a tour of the Far East, visiting China and Hong Kong. From the start, things didn't go to plan. On the plane journey over, I'd poked a steward in the back to ask him for a drink, only for it to turn into a skirmish. The pilot sent a message out, warning us he would stop the plane in Russia and leave us there, and it also led to an official complaint being made about my behaviour to the FA. I played well against China, providing a nice through ball for Nick Barmby to score his second goal, and then passing it into the net to get England's third. That was my first goal for my country since 1993, and I was made up. I missed the match against a Golden FC Select XI side in Hong Kong three days later due to an infected blister on my toe, which was probably just as well as we laboured to a 1-0 win and emerged with little credit.

Following the game, the gaffer allowed us to enjoy a night out before we flew home the next evening – which also happened to be my 29th birthday. His assistant Bryan Robson went along to keep an eye on things, which was a bit of a joke really, as he liked a drink and a laugh as much as anyone, and we were told we had to be back by 2.30am. Some of the sensible lads stayed in the hotel, but a large group of us ended up in a club called China Jump. Robbie Fowler and I got into some light-hearted pushing and shoving, which ended with me pouring a pint over his head. Then I did the same to Teddy Sheringham and Steve McManaman. I also ripped Steve's T-shirt by accident. All of a sudden, we'd created a new game for the night – everyone had to have their shirt ripped and a pint tipped over their head. I even did it to Bryan Robson, who was wearing one of his best shirts. It just came away in my hands, leaving the England assistant manager standing there wearing only a shirt collar.

As the night wore on, someone suggested we make use of the dentist's chair, a fixture in the club, where barmen would pour spirits down your throat while you sat back with your mouth wide open. At least eight of us gave it a try, having tequila and vodka poured into our open mouths, with most of it ending up on our torn clothing. I think Steve Howey won the competition, another Geordie who liked a laugh. And that was it, we went home relatively early. I shared a taxi back to the hotel with Bryan Robson and everything seemed to be okay.

It wasn't until a few days later, when photos taken of us in the club were plastered all over the papers, that it exploded into a major story. On their front page *The Sun* described me as a "drunk oaf with no pride," while other reports demanded I be thrown out of the squad. It was another example of the press trying to stitch us up in the run up to a major tournament, just like they had done in Italia '90. All it did was bring us closer together and it instilled an "us against them" attitude that we used as extra motivation. Terry Venables was completely behind us, he knew the real story and how it had been blown out of proportion by the media reports – although, yes, the pictures did look bad.

What made the situation even worse was an incident which took place on the flight home from the Far East. It had been a tiring trip and, having had a few drinks, I soon fell into a deep sleep, only to be woken by somebody giving me a massive slap across the face. I was enraged, demanding to know which bastard had done it. Nobody would own up, so I took vengeance on the whole cabin, throwing cushions around, punching TV screens, kicking seats. We were on the top deck of the Cathay Pacific plane, and before too long an FA official came from the cabin below asking us to keep the noise down. "Fuck off," I told him. "Don't you dare tell an England player what to do."

When we landed, there was trouble brewing. There was a bill of £5,000 to pay for two broken TV monitors, and the FA were demanding the culprit be excluded from the squad. Our captain, Tony Adams, pulled us all together and made it clear if one of us was being forced out of the squad, we would all go. Not only that, the whole squad would share the bill for the smashed-up TVs. "Collective responsibility" was the phrase used, and I was massively grateful to Tony and all the other players for agreeing to it – even Alan Shearer, the bastard who had slapped me in the first place.

Terry Venables made it clear, though, that some FA officials had wanted me thrown out, so I owed it to everyone to repay their support. I'd like to think that I did that as the tournament progressed. I was so anxious ahead of the first game, I started to worry that I might not be in the starting XI. It got so bad that I had to speak to the boss about it, who quietly assured me that I would be playing, which made me feel much better. We didn't get off to the best of starts, though, drawing 1-1 with Switzerland, who everyone expected us to beat with ease.

The next match was against our old rivals Scotland, and the Rangers lads had been hammering me for months, saying they were going to give us a good hiding. I really wanted to do well in this match, I'd been anticipating it for months. I was so excited that Bryan Robson was forced to raid the medical supplies and build a makeshift fishing rod for me, the day before the match. I ended up sitting next to the bath in the Burnham Beeches hotel, pretending to fish. It was the only thing I could do to relax and take my mind off it all.

The Scotland game was a tight affair as there wasn't much between the two sides. Alan Shearer put us ahead early in the second half, but the turning point came when our goalkeeper David Seaman saved a penalty kick from Gary McAllister. Well-known TV psychic Uri Geller tried to take credit for it later, saying his mind powers had moved the ball fractionally before McAllister hit it. Bollocks to that, it was all down to Old Beaver Face Seaman, my fishing mate who I'd spend an occasional afternoon with, sitting by a river with rod in hand.

Within 60 seconds of David's save, I was bearing down on Scotland's goal. I managed to dink the ball over Colin Hendry's head with my left foot and then volley it with my right, sending it flying past my Rangers teammate Andy Goram and into the net. Years later, I bumped into Colin in London, and he asked: "Hey Gazza, what are you doing here? I thought you lived in Bournemouth?" I shot back at him: "What are YOU doing here? I thought I left you on the floor at Wembley?"

Before the game, I had encouraged the lads to do the dentist's chair celebration if we scored, so I ran straight to the side of the goal, lay down with my mouth wide open and waited for the others to join me. Lucozade had never tasted so good! And that, for me, was the moment when Euro '96 took off and the country went football crazy. 'Three Lions' became the new national anthem that summer – I played the song to death myself, in my hotel room and then on the coach to games – and the tune's chorus, "football's coming home", rang around Wembley endlessly from that moment onwards. And we had turned the scandal of the dentist's chair into a joke – the press had no choice but to eat their words and join the rest of the fans in supporting our efforts.

I used to sit next to Andy Goram in the Rangers dressing room, so I couldn't wait to get back for pre-season training when it was all over. My dentist's chair celebration had made a double page spread in the papers, so I photocopied the articles and stuck dozens of copies on the walls of the changing room. Andy didn't find it funny. "If you put any more of them up," he said, "I'll fucking strangle you." I didn't realise the Scots could be so touchy.

Our final group match was against Holland, and we produced the performance of our lives to thrash the Dutch 4-1. Terry Venables was a keen student of the Dutch game, and his team talk before the match ensured we were fully focussed, reminding us of how skilled and tactically astute they were. I was more concerned about my boots at the time, though. I'd just been given a boot contract by Adidas, but had somehow managed to leave my pair behind in the hotel – not realising until I'd reached the dressing room and opened my bag in a panic. The only other player with Adidas boots was Teddy Sheringham, so I begged him to lend me a pair. I wear a size nine, but all he had spare were an old pair of ten and a halves with a rip down the side. So I stuffed a pair of socks in them and just prayed they would last the game. Afterwards, having had one of the best games of my life, I thought: "I'll keep hold of these boots."

But Teddy wasn't having it, he grabbed them back and said: "I'll have them back, thanks. Oh, and will you sign them for me?"

We had made it into the quarter-finals, where we faced Spain. They were a good side, very skillful, and it was a hard-fought match. By the end of extra time it was 0-0 and so we faced our first competitive penalty shoot-out since that night in Turin in 1990. I hadn't taken a penalty on that occasion, as I was still too upset from getting my second booking, but this time I put my name forward and thankfully scored. I was especially pleased for Stuart Pearce, who had missed his spot kick back in 1990 but managed to exorcise his demons by hitting the net, as we emerged 4-2 winners on penalty kicks.

The Germans – who else – awaited us in the semi-final and just like in 1990 I feel we were the better team on the night. We took the lead after just two minutes when Alan Shearer got on the end of my corner kick, after Tony Adams had flicked the ball into the box. But the Germans fought back to 1-1 through Stefan Kuntz and the game went into extra time. The next team to score would win, thanks to the new golden goal rule that had been introduced.

We came close when Darren Anderton hit the post, and then shortly after it seemed certain I would score as Alan Shearer crossed the ball along the goal line. Had the roles been reversed and I had crossed to Shearer, he would have scored without any question, but I just hesitated slightly, thinking that the goalkeeper would parry the ball into my path, and when he missed I just couldn't reach to tap it in. It is the one moment of my career that I can't bear to watch back on TV, it's still too painful, almost 30 years later. We were literally a whisker away, and I had also been robbed of another crazy goal celebration –

Battleground: Getting to grips with Vinnie Jones, John Fashanu and Wimbledon's Crazy Gang in the FA Cup, 1988 *(above left and right)*

Head for heights: Climbing for a header for Newcastle v Sheffield Wednesday *(left)* and a photo with the rest of the Newcastle squad in the summer of 1986, just as I broke into the first team

Scissor hands: Giving Glenn Roeder a haircut with the help of expert Helen Coyle in 1986 *(left)*

Fundraising: At the Great North Run in 1986 *(above)* and a charity awards dinner for leukaemia in Byker, 1988 *(below)*

History makers: Winning the 1985 FA Youth Cup with Joe Allon *(right)*, the last time Newcastle lifted the trophy

Ball boys: The expression says it all as Vinnie Jones gets my attention, 1987

The biggest stage: Taking on Ireland at the 1990 World Cup, when my career really started to take off

Agony and ecstasy: Celebrating after playing a starring role in the 1991 FA Cup semi-final victory over Arsenal at Wembley *(left and above)*, before injuring myself in horrible fashion in the final weeks later *(above)*, a day that would end in a hospital bed

World in motion: Italia 90 was the tournament that changed my life; from facing Cameroon *(above)*, beating Belgium *(above left)*, heartbreak and tears against West Germany *(top)* and finally returning home a superstar *(above right)*

Joy: One of the greatest moments from my playing career, as I beat Colin Hendry before hammering in a volley against Scotland at Euro 96, then celebrating with a nod to the infamous dentist's chair story

North of the border: I loved my time at Glasgow Rangers, where I won plenty of trophies

New horizons: Making my debut for Lazio against Genoa in September 1992. Again, I had a brilliant time in Rome – I loved it there and the fans seemed to enjoy watching me!

Dizzy heights: Bursting through midfield against Switzerland at Euro 96 *(right)* and scoring in the Old Firm derby later that year *(below)*

Local hero: Another derby and another crucial goal, this time the very late equaliser for Lazio against Roma at the Stadio Olimpico *(left)*

Bossing it:
I managed
Kettering briefly
(above), but
there were a lot
of things about
the job that I
didn't enjoy

Family matters: With Katie
and her son Mason *(top
left)*, with Nancie, Katie's
little girl *(top right)*, and
the Gascoigne clan *(left to
right)* my niece Lauren and
her partner George, Katie's
friend Tosh, Katie holding
my great niece Halle, my
sister Lindsay, nephew Joe
and my sister-in-law Jane

Always a performer: Going
on stage to speak to my fans
(left) – something I really
love doing

I don't know what I would have done, but it would have been spectacular!

As it was, the match went to penalties – again – and, once more, the Germans won when Gareth Southgate missed the crucial kick. It was a horrible way to go out, worse than Italia '90 in a way because the whole stadium – the whole country – shared in our grief. I'd scored my penalty again – despite changing my mind at the last minute – but that was no consolation. All we could do was return to our hotel and drown our sorrows.

To take my mind off the terrible defeat, I got into some high jinks with Robbie Fowler, and we started squirting tomato sauce at each other. It ended with me going into the kitchen, finding a huge carton of red sauce and then pouring it all over him. It sounds childish, but other lads played far worse practical jokes on me that night. Steve Stone, the Forest midfielder who went to Heathfields school like me, went as far as having a shit in my bag. Steve Howey pissed in it too, and the worst part was I didn't find out about it for almost a month, as I went on holiday and got married straight after the tournament. Meanwhile my bag was festering horribly at home, so you can imagine the smell when I finally opened it.

It amazes and saddens me when I look back now, to realise how close we came to winning Italia '90 and Euro '96. We were better than the Germans on both occasions, and I'm certain we would have beaten Argentina in 1990 and the Czech Republic in 1996 had we reached the finals. We were just a couple of penalty kicks away from making history.

4
ANGER

PROLOGUE

ANGER – Characterised by feelings
of frustration, hostility or irritation
that arise from a perceived injustice,
threat or wrongdoing.

I DON'T GET ANGRY VERY OFTEN, WHICH I believe showed in the kind of football I played. I never challenged or tackled out of rage, unlike a lot of players, and I didn't lose my temper with the referee, no matter what decision he made. Overall, football brought me joy, and rarely made me angry. Ahead of a game, I'd be fizzing with excitement and sometimes I'd be sad afterwards, mainly because those precious 90 minutes were over, and especially if we lost. But I was hardly ever angry.

The anger, when it happened, was fuelled by decisions made off the pitch by management, or frustration with how we'd performed, if we'd played badly. Sometimes I'd have a bit of a go at the lads – there was the occasion I mentioned earlier when I called the Tottenham players "soft southern shites", for example, because it seemed to me they'd allowed the rain and the cold to put them off their game.

There was only one time I really lost it, and that was when England manager Glenn Hoddle booted me out of the squad ahead of the World Cup 1998 despite me playing a crucial role in us qualifying for that tournament. That was a truly devastating moment which saw me fly into a mad rage and tear his hotel room to pieces. I'd wanted to thump that bastard Hoddle for leading me to believe I was on the team, before dropping me like a hot potato. Thankfully, I managed not to resort to violence, but I was so worked up I was given valium to calm down. I guess it was in everyone's best interests to keep me sedated on that occasion.

It's no secret that people have been angry with me over the years, often unfairly I would argue, for my behaviour off the pitch. Sometimes I deserved their anger, but a lot of the time I didn't.

Someone I pissed off big time was Alex Ferguson (long before he was a knight of the realm), when I told him I was going to sign for Manchester United, only to do so with Tottenham Hotspur while he was on holiday. He went off it, did Fergie, and I guess you couldn't really blame him. I'll admit, I could have handled that situation differently.

These days Katie tells me I can be "aggy", especially when I am drinking, or afterwards, while I'm detoxing. "Stop being so aggy," she'll say to me. She's right, I do get a bit snappy, and I'll bite her head off, even though I know she's only trying to help.

It's the drink that does that. Sober, I don't get angry at all. What's the point? Life's far too short.

ALEX FERGUSON

AT THE END OF THE 1987/88 SEASON THERE WAS just one question on everyone's lips – "Gazza's leaving Newcastle United. Where will he go?"

The fans were desperate to find out, and it was all I was asked about both on the pitch and off – the interrogation was constant.

"Please don't sign with Manchester United," the supporters would beg. "They'll beat us 7-2 if you do that."

The problem was, I felt as though nothing was really happening at Newcastle United. We hadn't won a domestic cup for over 30 years, which was pathetic really.

Meanwhile, I was fast becoming the hottest property in football with every club in the country wanting my signature. I'd had a fantastic season at Newcastle, been crowned the PFA Young Player of the Year, and was on the cusp of the full England squad.

It also helped that Newcastle United legend Jackie Milburn

went on national TV and raved about me – I couldn't get over it when I heard it.

"I think it's about 35 years since I've seen a kid as good as what this lad is, and I just can't believe the skills of him. He's got everything, everything. He sticks out a mile," he said.

Then he added: "There's no holding him, he is the best in the world. Honestly – the best in the WORLD."

I just went: "Wow." I couldn't believe someone as special as Jackie Milburn thought so highly of me.

I knew Tottenham Hotspur were after me but initially I had no intention of going down to London, I thought I'd do better at a northern club. I really wanted to go to Liverpool, then the best team in the land. I had been in talks with their manager Kenny Dalglish, who seemed keen, but I was told the club didn't have the money. So when it came down to it, it was between Spurs and Manchester United and I really struggled to make my mind up. I was veering towards Manchester United, because I thought I would feel more at home there than down south.

The manager, Alex Ferguson, who I'd already been negotiating with, rang me up and said: "Gazza, I'm going on holiday tomorrow, but I really want you to sign with us."

I told him: "Don't worry, go on your holiday. When you come back, I'll be at Old Trafford."

Looking back, I'm not entirely sure why I said that as deep down, I think I did have my doubts even then. Anyway, while Fergie was on his hols and I was staying with my dad, Irving Scholar, chairman of Spurs, phoned me up

"We want to sign you," he told me.

I said: "Nah, I'm signing with Man U."

In the background, my dad was going: "Who is it, what do they want?"

"Hang on one minute," I told Irving.

"It's Spurs, Dad," I said. "They want me to sign with them."

"Tell them to fuck off," he replied. "You're signing with Man U."

I got back on the phone to Irving, who'd heard every word, and he said: "Tell your dad I will give him £120k if you sign for Spurs."

"Dad," I said. "Spurs will give you £120k if I sign with them."

He didn't have to think about it, my dad, he just told me: "Well, what are you waiting for then, son?"

I still couldn't make my mind up, though. I'd made a promise to Fergie, and it didn't seem fair to go back on my word. I told Irving I would think about it and put the phone down.

Then, my dad, who hadn't even moved from his chair, said: "Can I also have a BMW soft top, with a private reg?"

I called Irving back and asked. "No problem," he said.

I still had a few doubts, but the next thing I knew, Lindsay was on the phone.

"If my dad is getting £120k and a BMW, can I have a sunbed?" she asked.

"Fucking hell," I thought, but I got on the phone to Irving, once again, and he agreed, straight away. A sunbed was no problem at all.

My agent Mel Stein did try and get through to Fergie to see if he would match Spurs' terms, but reaching someone on the telephone when they were abroad was tricky back then, and he wasn't able to. So, in the summer of '88, the poor old sod came home to the news that I'd signed for Tottenham.

To be fair, it wasn't just the cash which attracted me to London, I was genuinely worried about the Newcastle fans, who meant the world to me. I knew they'd never forgive a move to Manchester United.

There was also the question of Bryan Robson and Norman Whiteside in midfield, who were both established, skilful players. I couldn't help but think: "Am I even going to get a game here?"

To add to my decision, my good friends Chris Waddle and Glenn Roeder, who'd both played under Terry Venables, manager of Tottenham, were convinced I'd love working with him. So that was that, for better or worse, my mind was made up.

Ferguson went fucking off it when he found out, and sent me a furious letter. "I believed you when you said you'd sign for Manchester United," he wrote. "You've made a big mistake."

I have no doubt he thought I was a double-crossing bastard and I know he's never really let it go, because he was still banging on about it quite recently, when Katie and I took the kids to see a Manchester United game at Old Trafford.

A steward came up to us as we sat in the stands and said: "Alex Ferguson wants to see you in his office."

Even then, at 80 years of age, he said: "Why didn't you fucking sign with me? Biggest mistake you ever made."

I still look back, even now, and wonder if I made the right decision all those years ago, it's only natural. But if I'd gone to Manchester United, I might have ended up staying there for 15 years, and never experienced playing abroad. As things turned out, I had an absolutely brilliant time at Tottenham, and what's done is done, I can't change it – even if it did make Fergie apoplectic with rage.

2

GLENN HODDLE & WORLD CUP '98

I WAS GUTTED WHEN TERRY VENABLES STEPPED down as England manager and was replaced by Glenn Hoddle in 1996. Terry had been a great pal and mentor, the best in the business, but I hadn't had much to do with Hoddle. He'd left Spurs as a player in 1987 – the year before I joined – and though I knew he'd had a brilliant football career, I wasn't sure I trusted him.

Both Terry and Rangers manager Walter Smith had said the exact same thing to me. "Be careful of Glenn Hoddle," they'd warned. "He'll want to make a name for himself."

I didn't quite understand what they meant, but for the two of them to have told me that separately was worrying.

Sure enough, I didn't get on too well with Hoddle, mainly because he treated us players like kids a lot of the time.

He got this French dietician to come and tell us how to chew our food properly, which had the lads in stitches. "Chew to win!" we'd yell in hysterics, which was this guy's catchphrase. Hoddle also tried to tell us how to stretch, which was ridiculous considering he was dealing with some experienced players who knew their bodies – what worked for them and what didn't – better than anyone.

The maddest thing he did was send us all to see his spiritualist healer, Eileen Drewery. Hoddle thought she would be able to cure me of my compulsion to drink and smoke. I was with her almost an hour, while she gently laid her hands on my head and body.

"You've got demons inside you," she told me. "I'm going to try and set them free."

Then, she opened the window to let them out and I couldn't help it – I got the giggles. I was imagining the evil spirits leaving my body, then making a beeline for her garden.

"What's wrong, Paul?" she asked.

"Sorry," I said. "It's the demons. They're pulling funny faces at the window."

I was snorting with laughter now, I had no control over it – this was one of the most bizarre situations I'd ever been in. Elieen didn't look impressed, or find my joke funny, and shortly afterwards she asked me to leave.

She told me: "Now, don't have a cigarette or beer tonight."

"OK," I said.

But once I'd gone, I glanced back at the house and I caught sight of her through a window, puffing away on a fag.

"What a load of bollocks," I thought. "I'm not listening to her."

Despite my misgivings about Hoddle, I was doing well on the

pitch – I'd played in every World Cup qualification game, and had helped England reach France '98, so I had no real concerns I wouldn't be on the plane for that year's World Cup. Hoddle had also stood by me after some photos of Sheryl appeared in the *Daily Mirror* with the headline, "GAZZA BEATS SHERYL BLACK AND BLUE," and I had been grateful to him for that.

More on that later…

I'll admit, there were a few unfortunate incidents in the lead up to the World Cup that didn't reflect well on me, but they were blown out of proportion and weren't really my fault.

On Friday, May 15th, I appeared on my mate Chris Evans' show *TFI Friday* on Channel 4, which was a right laugh. I was locked in a box with a sign which read: "Do not open until June 15, Tunisia v England." The joke was I was too important for anything to happen to me before England's first match, so I had to be protected at all costs. On my way to the box, the audience were cheering me on and handing me cigarettes, so I opened a pack and put three tabs in my mouth. It was only a joke, but I accept, in retrospect, it probably didn't reflect too well on me.

Afterwards, we went out for a few beers, as you do. It was nothing wild, just a couple of drinks with a pal. Then, on my way back to Chris' house at around 1.30am I decided to get a kebab. That was my only mistake, really, to be stupid enough to be seen in public eating fast food in the early hours of the morning. Kebabs have a bad reputation as the grub you shovel into your mouth after a night on the piss to soak up the booze, which is unfair in itself.

The kebab in question was chicken, full of protein, which is exactly what's needed when you're training hard and working on your fitness. But try telling that to Glenn Hoddle, the papers and the England fans!

Unfortunately, someone had managed to get a picture of me scoffing the kebab, which was delicious by the way, and the next morning I was all over the tabloids, alongside a load of commentary about how I wasn't taking my fitness seriously enough and should be dropped from the squad.

Instead of defending me, Hoddle told the press: "I've said to Paul that mentally and physically you have to keep your body in shape.

"It's not just coincidence that he's ended up getting injuries. He's got to understand that a lot of the injuries are because his body might not be in good shape."

It struck me as grossly unjust, because I knew for a fact that a group of England players had been out in Soho that same night until 4am. They were lucky to have avoided being seen, that's all, while I was demonised yet again, but at least Chris stuck up for me. On his Virgin Radio breakfast show on Monday morning, he called for a "Get Behind Gazza" campaign, and said: "Paul is one of the most professional sportsmen – when he is working – that you could ever come across, ever, and he will train harder than anybody else."

He described me as "totally sober" and added: "It was about 1.30am. That's a reasonable hour for a man of 31 to go home at the weekend on his day off."

Thanks, Chris! But, I'll admit, it wasn't a particularly good look in the run-up to the World Cup, and I'd been spotted out with Chris and Rod Stewart, also a mate, on another occasion as well, but the whole thing was exaggerated to a ridiculous extent.

I didn't think I was playing too badly, which was the most

important thing and towards the end of the month there were a series of friendlies ahead of the big tournament. On May 27th, which happened to be my 31st birthday, England beat Morocco 1-0 in Casablanca, with Michael Owen scoring the winning goal. I played the full 90 minutes in the searing African heat and I was pleased with my performance. It's true, I was a bit distracted as there were stories in the papers about Sheryl being in a new relationship, which I was gutted about. It was difficult, but I never let what was happening off the pitch affect my ability to play football, despite what Hoddle and others said at the time.

We flew to our training camp in La Manga, Spain, after that game and as it was my birthday, I'm afraid I'd had a few drinks, and I was ten minutes late for the bus which was taking us to the airport. We still made the flight, it was nothing really, but Hoddle was absolutely seething and everyone knew it. Two days later we took on Belgium, but unfortunately I got a dead leg after 50 minutes and I had to come off. We lost that game on penalties after a 0-0 draw.

Hoddle looked gutted as I limped towards him and he told me: "I need you fit for France. We won't be able to do this without you. Please, will you just be careful. You need to look after yourself."

The guy was practically begging me to recover in time and as a result I naturally believed I'd be in the squad, I had no reason to doubt it. We returned to La Manga, where Hoddle would soon choose his England squad of 22 out of a total of 28 players he'd flown to the camp.

Two days after the Belgium game, on Sunday May 31st, we were told to relax, play golf, lounge around the pool, do whatever we wanted, but the mood was tense. We were all on tenterhooks as we waited to find out which of us would be going home.

That day, I noticed that there was a line of players standing in the corridor outside Hoddle's room.

"What are you doing?" I asked them. "Standing in a queue, like kids?"

"We've been asked to go and see him, one after another, to find out if we're in," a player told me, I forget which one.

"How dare he," I spat. "He's treating us like children. Why doesn't he just tell us? There's no way I am waiting around like this."

I barged into another room, where Glenn Roeder, my old mate from Newcastle United, who was now an England coach, was sitting with assistant manager John Gorman.

"Go on, then," I demanded. "Am I in or not?" I'd been good friends with Glenn for a very long time by that point, and just one glance at his face told me what I needed to know. He looked absolutely gutted, and I realised there and then, with sickening certainty, I hadn't made the England squad and I wouldn't be going to France with the rest of the lads.

I don't know if I have ever felt rage and sorrow like it as I struggled to process the enormity of what was happening. I was 31 years old, which meant the chances of me playing in a World Cup again were virtually nil.

"That absolute bastard," I thought to myself.

It wasn't the fact I'd been dropped, though there was that as well, it was the way Hoddle had gone about it. He'd led me to believe I was going to be in the squad, and then he had us all standing there like kids, waiting our turn to see him. I wasn't having it.

I stormed into his room and started yelling at him.

"Calm down," he told me. "Let's just talk."

"No!" I shouted.

The last thing I wanted to do was sit quietly, while he gave me his reasons for letting me go. In a blind rage, I smashed up his TV, threw his lamps on the floor, hellbent on trashing his room. I stopped short of launching a punch at Hoddle, but that's not to say I wasn't sorely tempted.

"Let me explain," he said.

"You absolute bastard!" I yelled. "Just shut the fuck up!"

In the end, David Seaman and Paul Ince burst in and restrained me, otherwise God knows how much more damage I would have caused.

I was given some valium to calm me down and sent to my room, but now I knew I hadn't made the squad, all I wanted to do was go home.

On the plane to London, along with Phil Neville, Nicky Butt, Ian Walker, Dion Dublin, and Andy Hinchcliffe, the other players who hadn't been picked, I was in tears. I kept thinking about what Walter Smith and Terry Venables had said to me – "Watch Hoddle. He is trying to make a name for himself." Those words had definitely come back to haunt me.

Sheryl and I were in the process of getting divorced but it was her house in Hertfordshire I returned to in an absolute state. I wanted to be with my family, even though things were just as much a mess on that front as they were on the pitch.

It was fucking mayhem outside the house, with dozens of TV crews and photographers camped out on the road. We tried to shield Regan, who was only two, but the camera bulbs flashed right in his eyes, and he started screaming his head off.

I remember standing in the garage at Sheryl's house, bawling my eyes out. I was absolutely devastated.

Meanwhile, the country was gripped by World Cup fever and I couldn't stand it.

I decided to take the whole family and some mates to Miami in Florida, to get away from everything. I knew the Americans weren't going to be watching the World Cup and, I won't lie, it was also an excuse to hit the drink, to try and forget my worries. By the time I got home, it was all over and done with.

I'd never warmed to Hoddle, and something which made me chuckle slightly during that difficult time was the memory of him flying out to Italy, while I was playing for Lazio, to try to get me to sign for Chelsea.

There was absolutely no way a move back to London was on the cards, but I still allowed him to take me out for a decent fucking lunch, and pay for the lot.

I remember I had a slack tooth that day, and it fell out of my mouth as I bit into my sandwich, while Hoddle, who'd just become Chelsea manager, tried his best to poach me from the Italians. But I was too busy looking for my tooth to pay any attention to what he was saying, and I was never going to go anyway.

I did come to terms with being dropped eventually and if I'm honest it helped that we were knocked out by Argentina in the last 16. I was rooting for the lads, but I think I would have found it more difficult to deal with if they'd managed to go all the way without me.

Footballers, including David Beckham, and fans alike widely speculated the outcome might have been different had I been in the squad.

EIGHT

No-one will ever know for sure, though I often wonder what would have happened had I been allowed to play. But anyway, it was all a long time ago. I bumped into Hoddle in a hotel lift, a few years later.

"How are you?" he asked me.

"I'm alreet, mate," I told him, and we both smiled.

5 SADNESS

PROLOGUE

SADNESS – Pain associated with feelings of loss, despair, grief, helplessness, disappointment and sorrow.

I'M SITTING ON THE ROADSIDE, CRADLING THE body of a dying boy in my arms. His limbs are twitching slightly, giving me hope he's alive, but then he becomes still and I know for certain he is dead.

If someone were to ask me when sadness entered my life for the first time, I would tell them it was the day little Steven Spraggon was knocked over and killed on Derwentwater Road, in Gateshead, while I was supposed to be taking care of him.

"Please move, please move!" I pleaded with his lifeless body, but it was too late, he'd gone.

I will never be sure, but if it wasn't for that tragedy, which left me with a guilt I carry to this day, I do not know if the addictions

I struggled with in my later years would have taken hold in the way they did. Nothing was ever really the same after that.

It was following the death of Steven that I developed little twitches and tics, along with the uncontrollable urge to make loud noises. I'd just about manage to get these impulses under control, then Anna or Carl would taunt me by saying: "Look at me!" and do an imitation of a tic or twitch, starting me off again. They were only taking the piss, but it was a nightmare for me, leading to weeks or even months of peculiar movements.

I also developed obsessive compulsive disorder, and became preoccupied with cleanliness, certain numbers, and the Lord's Prayer. It was as though my brain was constantly anticipating danger, desperately coming up with ways of keeping me safe.

Later in life, I started drinking heavily just to quieten the noise inside my own head, as it was the only thing that brought me peace. But alcohol was also the very thing which led me to the depths of despair and pushed me to the brink of suicide.

Standing on the platform of Stevenage Station after drinking 36 hot toddies – yes, you read the right, 36 whiskeys – I'd never been as close to ending it. "All it takes is one little step at the right time, and everything will be over," I thought to myself.

I called my ex-wife Sheryl on that occasion, and she managed to talk me round, but over the years we caused each other an enormous amount of sadness. I've only ever had one long-term relationship and that was with Sheryl, who I still love to this day. But it was a tumultuous partnership and over the years we were apart more than we were together. I know from things that Sheryl has said publicly that she remembers some situations differently to me, which of course is fair enough.

The other big love of my life, of course, was football, and

when my career began to decline before it ended for good in 2005 I was bereft. Football was all I knew, and its absence left me with a void only booze and drugs could fill.

Doubled over at the side of the pitch, in the humidity of Guangdong province, China, I was convinced I was going to die. I was suffering from a terrifying panic attack just minutes before I was due to train with second division club, Gansu Tianma. I was Paul Gascoigne, I'd appeared 57 times for England, feted as one of the greatest players my country has ever produced, and here I was, shaking in my boots, worried I wouldn't be able to keep up with the lads in a lower league team.

"How the mighty fall," I thought to myself, lighting a fag, and trying my hardest to pull myself together.

I didn't know it then, but within two years I would have stopped playing, and would never kick a football professionally again. It's an understatement to say that made me sad. To this day, I find it too painful to watch football on TV most of the time, or to talk about it with others, which is a problem because it's the only thing a lot of people want to discuss.

The intensity of my sadness is perhaps why I feel this emotion so keenly in others, and always try my best to alleviate it.

Walking the streets of Poole in the middle of the night, I am on the lookout for anyone who appears down on their luck – homeless lads draped in dirty blankets, drug addicts, drunks. They startle when they realise who I am, as I hand them as much cash as I can spare and say: "If you tell anyone, I want this money back."

I hate sadness, in myself and in others, but I can't deny it's been a major part of my life, and despite the many joys I am grateful for today, it's always there just beneath the surface. I don't know if I'll ever get rid of it completely.

1

STEVEN SPRAGGON

"YOU'RE NOT COMING WITH US, STEVEN," MY mate Keith Spraggon told his little brother. "Just stay here."

As a lad, Keith, who I played football with at Redheugh Boys' Club, was my best friend. He lived close to our house in Dunston and we saw each other all the time.

When we were ten, there was a shop we'd often go into and, kids being kids, we'd take the piss out of the woman who worked there. We'd try to nick the sweets, and she'd chase us away. Needless to say, there wasn't a lot to do in Gateshead, and it was how we entertained ourselves.

On this particular morning, Keith didn't want his little brother Steven, who was just six, to come with us to the shop.

Steven was really begging, saying: "Mam said I could come."

But Keith replied: "Well, if you're coming, I'm staying here."

I felt sorry for the little lad. "I'll take you," I told him.

His mam Maureen said: "Look after him, Paul." I promised

her that I would, and we both ran to the shop, which was only about 100 yards away.

When we got there, we started messing around as we usually did, causing bother, when I said to Steven: "Quick, let's go."

He was just a few steps ahead of me, but he ran out in front of a parked ice cream van, and was hit by an oncoming car. His little body was thrown about 30ft into the air, and his shoes flew off. I rushed over to him and pulled him onto my lap. I could see his lips moving, and his body was twitching a little bit.

"Thank God, he's alive," I thought to myself, but I was wrong. Those little twitches were the last movements he ever made. There was nothing I could do, I just had to sit there, holding his body, waiting for the ambulance and his mam to arrive.

I will never forget Steven's mother, running down the road, screaming and screaming, with no shoes on her feet. I blamed myself for little Steven's death, even though his mam and Keith never did.

I spent a lot of time with Keith in the aftermath. I went over to his house, not realising Steven's body was in a coffin in his bedroom.

"Come on, let's go and see him," Keith said. "Pick him up, give him a cuddle."

I did as I was told, holding Steven's cold little body in my arms for a second time.

After the funeral, I spent about a week sleeping at Keith's house in the room where Steven's coffin had been. The tics and twitches I developed started soon after Steven died. I'd also headbutt the walls with such force I'd leave holes behind and it got so bad, Mam took me to see a psychiatrist.

There was a sandpit in the room, and he said to me: "I'd like you to sit in there, and play with the sand."

As a lad of ten, I was beyond embarrassed to be seeing a psychiatrist in the first place, especially one who made me mess about with sand.

"Sand, what's sand going to do?" I thought. "My best friend's little brother has just died in my arms."

After the appointment I turned to my mam and said: "Please, never take me there again."

"OK, son," she replied.

We never went back, and I didn't get any other help for the tics, or the trauma of that accident which killed little Steven Spraggon. I don't blame anyone for that, it was just the way things were back then. If it had happened today, I would have been offered all kinds of counselling.

The death of Steven marked a turning point in my life, changing me permanently from a happy-go-lucky lad to a fearful, anxious kid, and nothing was ever quite the same again.

2

SHERYL

I'M IN A FANCY WINE BAR SOMEWHERE IN Hoddesdon, close to where I live in Dobbs Weir, Hertfordshire, when I spot her – the woman who will become the major love of my life. She is absolutely stunning, with long blonde hair, and she is wearing a tiny miniskirt while chatting to her mate without giving me a second glance.

The eyes of pretty much everybody else in that bar are upon me, as the young lad who a few years earlier, in 1988, signed for Tottenham Hotspur for £2.2million, a record transfer fee at that time.

There are lots of girls in that bar, but this one stands out a mile, and so I walk over to her and ask her if she wants a drink.

"What's your name, love?"

"Sheryl," she replies.

"How are you doing?" I ask.

"OK," she says, not looking too impressed. I'm drunk by this stage, and messing around, and she probably thinks I am a bit of an idiot.

Sheryl's friend knows exactly who I am and asks: "Can I have your autograph for my little boys? I have three at home, and they are all football mad."

"Of course, doll," I reply.

At the end of the night, Sheryl turns to me and says: "I had no idea who you were, you know."

By 1991, I was one of the most famous blokes in the country, on the front pages of all the papers, and I thought to myself: "The whole world knows who I am!"

Just a year earlier I had made global headlines when I cried during the semi-final of the 1990 World Cup and I'd been mobbed ever since. The country was in the grip of Gazzamania, which meant I couldn't go anywhere without all hell breaking loose.

But I don't say anything, as I worry I'll come across as an arrogant bastard. Instead I ask for her number, and am delighted when she hands it over.

I keep in touch with her and she tells me she's going through a tough time, she's in the process of divorcing her husband and has two little kids at home.

"I'll show you some fun," I tell her.

I wasn't put off by her situation at all – she was good company, a bit timid around me, but most girls were, to be fair.

We started seeing each other regularly, spending a lot of time in hotels, to avoid the press, and it was a lot of fun to begin with. The chemistry between us was electric, and I could tell she liked me just as much as I liked her. I met her kids, Mason, then two, and Bianca, five, fairly early on.

Mason was too young to know who I was but at breakfast one day, Bianca stared and stared at me.

Eventually she said: "Mum, why is Gazza in our house?"

I was all over the TV and papers in those days, so it must have been strange for Bianca, coming down the stairs to find me in her kitchen.

Sheryl and I had been going out for about a year when I signed for Lazio, in Italy. The relationship had its ups and downs, and we did argue a lot, even in the beginning. I can't even remember exactly what we fought over now, but we could both get jealous, and I was away a lot, playing football, or training.

When I told her I was leaving Tottenham to go to Rome, her reaction shocked me.

In my mind, we were in quite a casual on-off relationship so I was surprised when she said: "You can't just go! The kids think you're their dad."

I thought this was a bit much, given I'd spent hardly any time with them and we'd been together for such a short amount of time, but I did have strong feelings for Sheryl and I suppose a big part of me must have wanted to make it work.

So, despite my misgivings, Sheryl came out to Italy to live with me. It was decided that Bianca, then aged about six, would stay at school, live with her dad and visit for holidays, while Mason and Sheryl would join me in Rome.

I'm afraid it was far from a success, Sheryl and Mason living with me in Italy. I was under a lot of stress while I worked to establish a name and reputation for myself at a new club. Then, I'd come home, and the house would be chaotic, and filled with the noise and mess of a toddler.

Sheryl and I were constantly at each other's throats, and I didn't really know how to be a dad to Mason. That wasn't his fault at all but entirely because I was so young myself, and completely focused on football, which I had to be – I was training harder than I had in my life.

We'd never lived together in Hertfordshire, and I wasn't used to being in a family unit.

I'm an impatient bastard at the best of times, and the sound of children crying would drive me mad. I got off a bus once, and walked about ten miles, just because a baby was wailing its head off.

It's fair to say I struggled living with young kids, while also concentrating all my efforts on performing at Lazio. Perhaps it was cruel, looking back, but I bought a few devices to put in their bedrooms which omitted a spooky "oooooooo" sound every time they made a noise.

One night Sheryl said: "Those kids are so quiet, they're not normally like this."

I didn't let on that it was because the poor mites were too scared to so much as whimper. Anyway, needless to say, it didn't work out, living with Sheryl in Italy. I was training twice a day, she didn't know the language, and my great big villa was in the countryside, away from everything.

I had grown to love those kids as my own and I still do to this day but it was a difficult time. I was probably a bit possessive when it came to Sheryl, and I didn't really like her going out and doing her own thing.

After about six months, Sheryl moved back to Hertfordshire and came over every so often for little breaks, holidays, with the kids.

We were apart a lot and one of the main sources of my anger towards Sheryl was my paranoia that she was involved with other men, fuelled by false stories in the papers.

I'm a very jealous guy, I'll admit that, and there's no cure for jealousy. You have a headache, you take a pill, but there's no magic drug for the green-eyed monster.

Sheryl always denied there was any other man and besides, we were constantly breaking up, and living separately most of the time anyway.

So, I'm not saying she would have been doing anything wrong, even if the stories were true, which I now realise they weren't.

But that didn't stop me from feeling sick with envy whenever the thought crossed my mind.

In the summer of 1995, at the end of my final season with Lazio, I was in the car with Sheryl when she said: "Paul, I have something I need to tell you. I am pregnant."

I know I should have been delighted by the news, but I just wasn't and I'll admit, I wasn't very kind to Sheryl about it. I didn't handle it well and I even wondered if the child was mine. My move to Rangers from Lazio was also very much on my mind, and I didn't want anything to distract me from my football.

We went on holiday after she told me the news, to Italy and Las Vegas, but Sheryl and I weren't getting on, and so I didn't really enjoy myself.

When we returned to the UK, Sheryl spent much of her time at her home in Hertfordshire, while I played for Rangers.

Our son, Regan, was due in February 1996 and shortly before his birth I was in London with the Rangers team. We didn't have a game and it was time for a bit of fun, a chance to let our hair down. I had a night out with the other players, before turning up at Sheryl's house the following day, a little bit worse for wear.

I knocked on the door, but Sheryl's mother answered.

"I'm here for the birth," I told her.

"Sheryl is about to have the baby," her mum said. "She's going into the hospital."

"I'd like to go with her," I said.

"If you don't go now," she told me, "I'll call the police."

Feeling like I had no option, I climbed into my car, and thought: "Fuck it. I'll drive up to Newcastle, see my mates."

As I was driving, my agent Mel rang me and said: "You need to turn around. It's important you're there for the birth of your son."

"There's no point," I replied. "The last thing I need is the police on my case."

I headed to my dad's house in Dunston, and then went out drinking with my friends, in a desperate bid to blot everything out. The next day, I went back to the pub and was sitting there when one of my mates opened up the *News of the World* and almost choked on his pint.

"Paul, there's a story about your son in here, look!" he said.

I grabbed the paper from him, and was confronted with a double page spread, about how Sheryl was in labour with a little boy she planned to call Regan.

That's how I learnt the name of my own son, from the bleeding *News of the World*.

I returned to Hertfordshire, and finally got to hold my little lad in my arms, which was wonderful. Despite my misgivings about becoming a father, I'd never felt love like it. It was absolutely brilliant.

The arrival of Regan, which Sheryl explained means Little King, brought the pair of us closer together. Despite our differences, we decided to try and make a go of things for the sake of our boy and Sheryl chose a beautiful house for us to live in, in Kilbarchan, Scotland. It was called The White House, of all things, and had a swimming pool, tennis court and six bedrooms.

"Wow, look at that!" I said to Sheryl, when we went round to view it, seeing pictures on the wall of the guy who owned it sitting in 10 Downing Street.

We all moved in together, Sheryl, Mason, Bianca, Regan and me, and were a proper little family for a while. We were happy, and getting on well, for the first time in ages.

There was no big, romantic proposal, or anything like that, but at some point we decided to get married.

The truth was, I was terrified that if we didn't, we'd break up, and I wouldn't be able to spend time with Regan. Looking back, I'm not sure I married for love, though I did love Sheryl, but out of a sense of duty.

In July 1996, Sheryl and I had a lavish wedding at Hanbury Manor, near Ware, in Hertfordshire, which cost £150k, a lot of money back then. Thankfully, the whole thing was covered by the exclusive media rights we gave to *Hello!* magazine.

Facing Sheryl at the altar of the chapel in front of all our family and friends, including England teammates David Seaman, Paul Ince, Chris Waddle, Ian Wright and pals Danny Baker and Chris Evans, was terrifying.

I was hyper aware of my relatives on one side, and Sheryl's on the other, all of them waiting for the moment we said: "I do."

When it arrived, both of us pledging to love and honour each other for all of time, I heard a distinctive "yes", whispered fiercely and triumphantly, from Sheryl's part of the church. I sneaked a glance at my own relatives on the other side, only to see Anna and Lindsay, sitting next to each other, silently crying.

I know lots of people weep at weddings, but their tears struck me as sad, not joyful.

It was at that moment, the very instant we made our vows to each other, that I knew I'd made a mistake. Straight away, I felt trapped, like this was not the right path for us to take, but there was nothing I could do then, it was too late, and I just had to make the very best of the situation and put on a brave face.

Don't get me wrong, there were good times with Sheryl, and I did love her. I'll never forget going to Disney World in Florida, sitting on the swings as darkness began to fall, laughing with her as we discussed all the old films from our childhood – Donald Duck, Popeye and Mickey Mouse. But for most of our relationship we were at loggerheads, even during our honeymoon in Maui, Hawaii.

We did try to make it work, and even went as far as going to marriage counselling with celebrity therapist Beechy Colclough, who'd also treated Elton John and Michael Jackson, but needless to say, that didn't end well.

We'd walk in arguing, and then come out double arguing, and the cost of it was absolutely mental, £10k or something, for an hour of talking.

"We're not going back there, darlin'," I told Sheryl.

Just three months into our marriage, in October 1996, the

disharmony between us erupted into a terrible episode I will regret for the rest of my life.

We were on a little break at The Gleneagles Hotel close to Perth, in Scotland, ahead of Rangers taking on Ajax in the Champions League, with the kids.

I started to argue with Sheryl over something stupid while we were having food in the restaurant.

She went upstairs to the hotel room, and I followed her there and put my head against hers. Instinctively, I pushed her away from me, throwing her to the floor.

"Fuck off," I told her.

As she landed on the floor she hurt her hand, and cried out in agony. I knew I'd well and truly fucked up on this occasion and once she'd calmed down, I left. There was nothing left for me to do or say.

A few days later the headline of the *Daily Mirror*'s front page story read "GAZZA BEATS SHERYL BLACK AND BLUE", and there were pictures of Sheryl outside the hotel, with her arm in a sling.

It's only fair I mention at this point that Sheryl's recollection of what happened is very different from my own.

Regardless, I will always be sorry for the pain I caused Sheryl that night, and I am sure a lot of people will believe I fully deserved what happened next.

"Wife beater, wife beater," rival fans would chant at me on the football pitch, or in the street, everywhere I went. Rangers came under pressure to drop me, and I was really grateful that manager Walter Smith stuck by me and I remained on the team.

Thankfully, that season was brilliant for the club. I played in 34 games and scored 17 goals as we won the Premier Division for the ninth season in a row, as well as the League Cup.

But the Gleneagles episode cast a dark shadow over my life and things between Sheryl and I were never quite the same again, despite brief spells of reconciliation.

The divorce finally came through in 1998, and despite everything, I was devastated.

It also took a huge financial strain as the settlement was £700k plus £10k a month in maintenance, which would become increasingly hard to find as my career began to dwindle.

Despite everything, and the huge amount of sadness we caused each other, Sheryl remains the great love of my life and the only woman I've ever had a long-term relationship with.

I'd rather be with my mates playing pool, dominoes and darts than go out with a girl, I've always been like that. I am scared to date a woman now as I find it so difficult to put my trust in someone.

To this day, I still think of Sheryl now and again, especially after I've spent time with Regan, and I find myself calling her when I've had a drink but she doesn't even answer and I don't blame her.

She rings me up sometimes herself, normally when I am poorly and in hospital.

"How are you doing?" she'll ask. "I'm alreet," I'll reply.

Sometimes, I fantasise about what it might be like if we got back together, but then I quickly talk sense to myself. "Don't even go there, Gazza," I think. But the truth is, regardless of the sadness our relationship caused to us both, I really loved Sheryl, and I always will.

REGAN

"BLOODY HELL, SON," I TOLD REGAN. "WE'VE been on that rollercoaster 22 times, and you want another go?"

"Dad, if you love me, you'll say yes," he replied, looking at me with beseeching, six-year-old eyes.

Well, Jesus Christ, what do you say to that?

Holding Regan's little hand, we bypassed the queue with our VIP tickets and walked straight on to Big Thunder Mountain – for our 23rd ride. The pair of us were on a trip to EuroDisney Paris, and we were having a brilliant time – though I was feeling quite sick by this point.

At the end of the day, I was exhausted, and I won't lie, as we made our way back to the hotel I did my best to avoid any attractions I thought he might want to go on.

But all of a sudden he spotted an ice rink. "Please, please, Dad," Regan said. "Can I go on?"

"OK," I sighed, and we picked up some boots.

EIGHT

I stood at the edge of the rink and watched him. "Be careful!" I yelled. "Your mam will kill me if you hurt yourself."

I was already in trouble with Sheryl over an incident involving a Bucking Bronco. Regan had impressed me by staying on longer than anyone else – but then I realised his foot was stuck in the stirrup. He eventually flew off with his leg still attached to the bull!

"Don't tell your mam, son," I begged. Well, of course, he was on the phone to her straight away.

Anyway, I needn't have worried about Regan on the ice, as he took to the rink like a real pro. He weaved his way through the crowds of skaters, many of them stumbling and falling over, with elegance and speed.

"Wow," I thought to myself. "He's fucking brilliant!"

Fast forward 20 years and I am sitting in the audience of a TV studio in Watford, Hertfordshire, to watch Regan take part in ITV show *Dancing On Ice*.

I was overcome with pride as he performed a stunning routine to 'Singin' in the Rain' with his partner Karina Manta. When the camera panned over to me and Bianca I got really emotional.

I was on the edge of tears as I told presenter Holly Willoughby how much Regan had impressed me during the competition.

I wasn't at all surprised when he won the final after dancing to 'Step in Time' from the *Mary Poppins* film – an absolutely amazing achievement.

Without a shadow of a doubt, the best thing to come out of my relationship with Sheryl is our wonderful son.

In some ways, we couldn't be more different, but Regan is a professional dancer, which means we're both sportsmen, and we all know that takes a lot of hard work and dedication.

He's travelling the world at the moment, and I don't see him as much as I'd like, but he'll always be one of the most important people in my life. I miss him and it does make me sad I don't get to see him more often, but I am so glad we have a good relationship. Given what happened with his mam, things could so easily have turned out differently.

4

MIDDLESBROUGH & EVERTON

IF I HAD TO CHOOSE ONE PLAYER I LOVED MORE than any other, it would be Bryan Robson. He was my Maradona, my Pelé, my Best. I'll never forget watching him on *Match of the Day* when I was a kid, scoring a fantastic header while playing for West Bromwich Albion. He also looked great, wearing his big curly perm with panache, and I was obsessed. So, at the start of my career, it was a total thrill to play against him whenever Newcastle faced Manchester United. Later on, it was an honour to have him as my midfield partner during Italia '90.

When I first joined the England squad, he came up to me and said: "Look, I am coming to the end of my career, and you are starting yours. Leave the tackles to me, as I don't want you getting injured. I'll take the high balls, and the stitches that come with them, too."

Robbo had come back from broken legs, a broken collarbone, and countless serious injuries, so for him to voluntarily put himself at risk to protect me said everything about the man. I only wish I had taken notice – I might have avoided some of the 38 operations I underwent during my career.

I remember visiting him at home once, and eyeing up the impressive Caterham Super 7 Lotus on his drive.

"Can I buy that off you?" I asked him.

"Yeah, why not," he replied. "I hardly ever drive it."

I can't remember what price we agreed on, but when I turned on the ignition to drive it back to Newcastle it wouldn't start.

"How are you going to get that home?" he asked.

"Transporter truck?" I ventured.

Well, I ended up sitting in that car, on top of this great big fucking lorry, all the way from Manchester to Newcastle. It was brilliant.

I got into a spot of bother with it during a day on the go-karts with the Tottenham lads. Me being me, I was banging my kart into the other players' with as much force as I could muster. In the end the owner came up to me and said: "Fuck off – you're barred."

To get my own back, I went home and picked up my beloved Caterham Super 7, drove to the course, crashed through the fence and sped around the track a few times.

Unsurprisingly, Terry Venables was fuming when he found out. "You'll have to buy them a new fence," he told me, which I did.

Bryan left Manchester United in 1994, just as the club were starting their period of dominance, and he became player-manager of Middlesbrough, winning promotion to the Premier

League in his first season. They had a lot of star players at the time, with Fabrizio Ravanelli, Juninho and Emerson lighting up their new Riverside Stadium, but by 1998 they had been relegated again, and the superstars had all departed. When I joined them, in March of that year, Middlesbrough were absolutely desperate to get back into the Premier League.

My time at Rangers had reached a natural end. I'd really enjoyed my first two seasons there, but the final year was not the happiest for me. I was going through a divorce, worrying about being a target of the IRA after another flute playing celebration, which was idiotic of me, I admit, drinking five nights a week – it was the only way I could escape from the pressures and problems plaguing my personal life – and as a result I was not in the best of form. On top of that, Walter Smith had announced he was stepping down as manager at the end of the season, to be replaced by Dick Advocaat. Walter warned me that I probably wouldn't figure in the new manager's plans, and mentioned that Middlesbrough had shown interest in me.

I joined Boro in March 1998, for a fee of £3.45 million. The club was pushing for promotion and were due to appear in the League Cup final at Wembley the following week. I was excited to link up with Bryan Robson, though I'd now have to call him gaffer, as well as old pals like Paul Merson and Andy Townsend, who I started living with in a huge mansion in Seaham, County Durham. Bryan thought Andy would be a calming influence on me, but the gaffer started having his doubts when he learnt of my antics.

Off the pitch, I was bored as ever, and on one occasion I bought a jet-ski, which I couldn't wait to try out. I ended up about a mile off the coast, with huge waves crashing over me. "Shit," I thought, "maybe this wasn't such a good idea after all!" I was wearing a big woolly jumper and I fell off the jet-ski, which then started circling me while I was flailing around in the chilly North Sea. Somehow I managed to grab hold of it, and get back to safety. That was the last of the jet-ski.

I made an appearance in the League Cup final against Chelsea as a substitute, but we lost the game 2-0 after extra time, and I gave my runners-up medal to Craig Hignett, who had played in all the other games – he deserved it more than me. My priority was to regain my fitness ahead of the 1998 World Cup, and help win promotion. I played in six of the last seven games of the season, helping the team to five victories and a draw – enough to secure promotion back to the Premier League.

By the time pre-season training began for the 1998/99 season, I had enjoyed a lovely holiday, was prepared to knuckle down and I got myself into peak physical shape. The gaffer had a surprise for us as he walked into the training ground dressing room. "Right guys," he said, "The chairman, Steve Gibson, has just spent £250k on a new state-of-the-art team bus to take us to away games. It's brand new. It's got a satellite dish, TVs, fridge freezers and everything." My eyes lit up. "Fucking great!" I thought.

I waited until he wasn't watching, then sneaked out of the exit door. There it was outside, this gorgeous new coach. I walked up to the driver and told him: "Hey, mate. Bryan Robson wants to see you."

"What for?" he asked.

"I don't know. Just fucking go!"

As soon as he left, I jumped into the driver's seat. The keys were in the ignition so I started it up. I thought: "I'm going to take this into town and put some bets on for the lads." It was a monster vehicle, and the best feeling in the world to hear the wheels move beneath me.

I came to a T-junction at the training ground exit, where unfortunately I momentarily forgot I was driving a massive coach, not a little Mini. When I turned right I drove straight into a concrete bollard, leaving one side of the coach caved in and mangled. I'd only left the car park two minutes ago.

I ran up to the security man and handed him the keys. "You drove that," I told him. He went: "Did I fuck!"

The bus was wrecked, and it wasn't very long before Bryan Robson rang me up. "Gazza? Where is the fucking bus?" he asked.

He was actually very good about it, though I did have to pay for the damage I'd caused.

I'll admit, I was in a pretty bad place at this point in my life, after an unfortunate combination of events pushed me into the throes of alcoholism. 1998 was the year I was booted out of the World Cup squad, just a few months before Jimmy's cousin, David Cheek, died in the most tragic of circumstances. More on that later. I was not coping well, and started using sleeping pills and booze to get me through the days.

But despite my terrible mental state, Middlesbrough actually began the season quite well. I was playing fairly well and we were picking up some good results, until the October international break when a four-day stay in Dublin turned into a booze fest, which landed me in the Priory.

I was back playing for Boro by November 1st, and won Man

of the Match in a 1-1 draw with Nottingham Forest. We had a great spell after that, and by Christmas we were fourth in the league. We ended up finishing in ninth place that year, which wasn't bad for a newly promoted side, and I'd managed 29 appearances and three goals. Kevin Keegan had replaced Glenn Hoddle as England manager by that point, and there was speculation that I might earn a recall – but it never happened, for whatever reason.

The following season, 1999/2000, started well too, but then in February 2000 I caught Aston Villa's George Boateng with my arm in a challenge. It looked bad – even friends like Gary Mabbutt came out and criticised me – but the person who suffered the most was myself, as I had broken my arm, which kept me out of action for a large remainder of the season. It had been a disappointing campaign, and I felt a new challenge and change of scenery would do me good. Middlesbrough were good enough to offer me a free transfer, which led to me joining up with my old Rangers boss Walter Smith, who was now at Everton.

It was me who made the first move, contacting Walter while I was staying at a health farm in Bedfordshire, and I practically begged him to sign me. He and Archie Knox, his trusted assistant, grilled me for hours, but finally I was given a fortnight trial period, followed by a two-year contract. I was sorry to leave Bryan Robson, who had been incredibly supportive, but he was getting hammered in the press himself. Journalists were accusing him of being too lenient as a manager, so having me off his list of problems was probably the best thing for him too.

For the first few months, I did well at Everton. I was helping the team to victories, earning a few Man of the Match awards along the way, and my fitness was improving game by game. At St James' Park in October, I was applauded by the Geordies as I left the field after Everton defeated Bobby Robson's Newcastle side 1-0. It had been great to see Bobby again before the match, and I enjoyed having a laugh with him on the touchline as the other players warmed up.

But that proved to be the high point of my season, as a string of niggling injuries took a toll on my fitness. Depression set in when I was unable to play, which in turn led to me drinking more frequently – it was a vicious cycle. Meanwhile, the papers were constantly rehashing stories about me being a wife beater. I felt everything was spiralling out of control and I was powerless to stop it.

It reached the stage where Walter had to give me a massive bollocking, because I was drinking far too much. He gave me an ultimatum – either go to a clinic and get yourself sorted out, or leave the club now with a handshake. And that is how I made my first visit to the Cottonwood clinic in Arizona, costing me £21k and 28 days of my life.

Upon my return, I stayed sober for nine months and got myself match fit for the start of the 2001/02 season. As with the previous year, I got off to a good start – even scoring my first – and only – goal for Everton, against Bolton in a 2-2 draw. But yet again, I began struggling with injuries, especially my hernia. My body was starting to let me down, which was only natural considering I was nearing 35 and had endured a punishing career littered with injuries and operations.

An FA Cup sixth round defeat to Middlesbrough proved to be my last game for the club, and it also signalled the end for Walter Smith. I felt sorry for Walter as he had done a good job during his time there. He had been the main reason I'd wanted to sign for the club. And so with Walter's departure, once again, it was time to say farewell and look to the future.

5

END OF CAREER

"WOULD YOU MIND TAKING MY KIT AWAY TO get it cleaned?" I asked the apprentice in the dressing room at Burnley.

"No problem," he replied. "But you'll need to pay."

"What?" I said, flabbergasted. I'd never even had to think about where my stuff got washed before, it was all taken care of for me. But at Burnley I had to pay this apprentice £5 a week to clean my boots, and £20 a month to sort out my kit.

I joined the second-tier Lancashire team in March 2002, and it was my first real experience of a lower league club. Needless to say, I was shocked by the lack of facilities and it made me realise how lucky I'd been playing in the top divisions for the entirety of my career.

I was brought in by manager Stan Ternent to help out during important games, when the lads needed a boost, and I was paid £5k a week with an extra £5k per appearance, but in the end, I was miserable there. I didn't enjoy their football, which seemed to be mostly about kicking the ball as far as you could, and I only stayed two months, playing in just six games.

That year, 2002, was a terrible one for me, as I had to come to terms with an alarming fact – I just wasn't the same player I used to be. I was 35, I'd suffered some horrendous injuries during my career, and the truth was I just wasn't as fast as I had been in my youth. I still loved to train, but on the pitch, if I couldn't beat a guy, I'd think: "You fucker, five years ago I would have smashed you with my eyes closed."

My mind was as sharp as ever, and I still knew what I needed to do with the ball, but my body just wasn't responding in the same way any more. It was frustrating, to say the least.

Facing my opponent, I'd bark: "You're fucking lucky I am this age. Not so long ago I would have torn you inside out."

I used to beat three or four players in a row, but when you can't get the better of just one, you think: "Fuck me, what am I doing?"

In the privacy of my hotel, I'd break down in tears as I asked myself: "Why the fuck am I still bothering?" But I didn't want to give up, not completely, as I simply couldn't contemplate a life without football – the idea was incomprehensible to me.

After I left Burnley, I started training like a mad bastard and really I took things a bit too far. I moved back up to the North East and began working with Steve Black, the Newcastle Falcons rugby club fitness coach. I'd get to the gym at a stupid time in the morning, like 5am, and then after my session I'd go for an eight-mile run. I was barely sleeping, and lost a ton of weight, but people kept telling me how great I looked.

Inside I felt terrible, but I was pretty fit for a 35-year-old, and

I hoped I might be able to get at least one year with a decent enough club somewhere.

I decided I'd like to go abroad, where I wasn't as easily recognisable and I could get a bit of peace, away from everyone. Then, I started working with the agent and ex footballer Wes Saunders, who I'd played alongside at Newcastle, and he started making approaches to foreign clubs.

That's how I ended up in the most polluted city in the entire world – Lanzhou, in deepest China, while playing for Gansu Tianma, the worst team in the Second Division. Wes had managed to negotiate about £400k in total for a year-long stint with the club, and I felt optimistic as I flew out to Hong Kong with my dad and Jimmy Five Bellies in March 2003, excited to begin a new chapter in my life.

I'd been in the Priory for a week to prepare, but unfortunately I fell off the wagon at Heathrow Airport. Me and my dad were terrified of flying, and we fed off each other's fear, which made it even scarier for us both, so during that 13-hour flight I allowed myself a few drinks and we all arrived in high spirits.

That wasn't the best of starts, but I hoped things would improve once I started playing with the team. Lanzhou, which can get as cold as -19C, was in the grip of a bitter winter, and so I spent the first few weeks undergoing pre-season training in a town called Qingyuan, in northern Guangdong, which has a milder climate.

While I was there I got speaking to an American journalist who lived in the Lanzhou, and I asked her: "What's it like?"

"You blow your nose, and it's black," was all she could say.

"Fucking fantastic," I thought to myself.

I've travelled all over the world, but when I arrived in that city, I got the culture shock of my life.

Struggling to breathe the parched air, I looked around in astonishment at the live animals – frogs, snakes and rabbits – being sold from little stalls on the roadside.

The hairdresser was one chair in the middle of the road, with all manner of traffic zooming past. I got ripped off almost straight away when I bought a Rolex watch which turned out to be fake. I thought the seller had asked for 300 yuan, about £24, and believing that to be a bargain, I handed him the cash. Jimmy was laughing his head off, and took great delight in telling me: "He wanted 50 yuan, not 300, you daft bastard."

"I'm sure it's real," I said, starting to doubt it.

"It's not, man," said my mate Heps. Ah, well, I thought.

Every day we'd see a poor little badger in a cage, which we all felt sorry for.

"I'm going to buy that badger and set it free," said my dad.

"OK, then," I replied, watching as he went and bartered with the seller. He could be a silly bugger at times, my dad. He let the badger go almost immediately and it scampered off through the chaos of the city. I was convinced we'd never see it again, but the very next day, there it was, back in the cage. Maybe it was a different badger, but it looked the same to me.

Meanwhile, I was impressed by the team and the facilities at the club and was looking forward to training with the lads, but there was one small problem – I had totally forgotten I had agreed to be a coach as well as a player.

It dawned on me as the English-speaking physio started to talk to me about devising a programme.

"Shit," I thought to myself as I remembered, part of the reason I had agreed to go to Gansu Tianma in the first place was because they had offered me a coaching position.

"The team's got good technique," I blustered. "It just needs a bit more organisation."

Then I joked: "I can't believe it's me saying that."

As it happened, my tenure started spectacularly well, and I scored a goal in the 14th minute of my debut match, securing a 2-0 victory against Hailifeng.

That was a big deal for a team who hadn't won a game for the whole of the previous season.

My old mate Gary Lineker even featured the goal on *Match of the Day*, replaying the clip of me scoring and saying: "Someone staking a claim for a late call up to the England team."

I was enjoying the training and the football, but my problems started off the pitch when I was alone in my hotel room and I had time to think. I was also finding it difficult to concentrate on my own playing when I was a coach as well as a player and trying my best to help the other lads.

I was drinking heavily by this point, and my teammates were having to shield me from the press.

Waking up every morning, my nose would be bleeding and I'd be covered in dust from the filthy streets of the city.

I was getting through a bottle a day of a Chinese liquor called Baijiu, which is 100 per cent proof, but I still managed to get out of bed and train with the lads whenever I needed to.

Jimmy said to my dad: "He's drinking again, you know."

"Yeah," said my dad, "but watch him come back faster than everyone else."

He was right and all – the lads and I would go for a 5k run and I would be the first to finish by a whole ten minutes, although that was probably because I was gasping for another drink, to be fair.

Overall, though, my time in China was horrific, especially after my dad and Jimmy went home, and I was desperate to leave by the end. One day, while still in Qingyuan, I suffered a terrible panic attack ahead of a training session. Sitting at the side of the pitch, with my head in my hands, I struggled to breathe as I wondered how it had come to this.

Here I was, still a relatively young man, far from home, in an alien country, and it was clear as day to me now – I really was at the bitter end of my career.

I was surrounded by open green spaces and I could see majestic mountains in the distance, but despite all this, I felt trapped. The panic attacks didn't stop the whole time I was in China, in fact they got worse.

I'd only been at the club eight weeks, but that was eight weeks too long for me and by this point China was in the grip of the SARS epidemic – I saw that as the perfect excuse to leave and never come back.

When I arrived back in the UK I had around a year off, trying to take it easy, and it was in the summer of 2004 that I got an offer from what would become the last club I would ever play for.

Boston United chairman Jon Sotnick and manager Steve Evans approached me and asked if I'd be interested in a coaching role at the club, with some playing.

I really wanted to get my FA coaching badge, so I thought it would help with that and give me more options going forward.

They were in League Two when I joined them and I was offered £15K a month with extra cash if gates were over 3,500. I lived in a hotel in the centre of Boston while I was there, and I can't say I was happy. In the end, I didn't get to do much coaching, and I also had a bit of a problem with Steve Evans, who always seemed to be shouting at the players.

One day, a young lad missed the ball during training and Evans bellowed: "Run up and down – now, quickly!" I watched, stunned, as the player put his head down and started jogging around the pitch.

I didn't think it was right, humiliating the youngsters like that, and it made me realise how lucky I'd been. I'd never been treated like that, not even as a very young player at Newcastle United.

One day, there was a disagreement in the dressing room, and one of the lads turned to me and asked: "What do you think, Gazza?" Evans was right there in the room, but that didn't hold me back. I said exactly what I thought, which was: "Take no notice of him, he doesn't know what he's talking about."

I'd only been there for just over two months but there was no option but for me to leave after that, and I didn't feel bad about it either. I'd got Boston United loads of positive publicity, which I am sure is one of the reasons they signed me in the first place.

After that, I had a brief stint at Kettering Town as the manager, but that didn't last long either, 39 days to be precise. I felt desperately sorry for the players at that club, which I joined in October 2005, under owner Imraan Ladak.

I'd had little experience of non-league before then, with semi-professional players coming into training after spending long days at work as postmen and bricklayers. The lads were paid hardly anything and some of them had to travel six hours just to train.

While they were exercising, I'd order 24 pizzas for them to scoff, as I realised they must be starving, bless them. I don't think my assistant Paul Davis was too impressed, though, when I stopped training sessions mid-way through because the food arrived!

In the end, I lasted eight matches. We won our first game, a 1-0 victory over Droylsden, and we also notched up a couple more victories, but our mistake was to try and get the players to perform beyond their capabilities. We wanted them to play like Germany and Brazil, to keep the ball on the ground, and it was too much for them.

I wasn't in the best of health at the time, after suffering a neck injury while rehearsing for ITV's *Dancing On Ice*, which I subsequently had to pull out of, and I still didn't have my drinking under control, so it was a tough time. My mental state wasn't helped by the passing of George Best, which really upset me. But, in spite of it all, I loved working with the players, interacting with them and passing on advice, and I think they responded to me well. They even recreated my dentist's chair celebration after one goal, just for my benefit.

No, managing a team wasn't for me, I very quickly realised. I'd been brought in to get Kettering out of the sixth tier and by the time I left they were heading down towards the seventh, so depending on which way you looked at it, I'd achieved my aim!

But joking aside, the end of my career, and the deterioration of my fitness, is one of the great sorrows of my life and what makes it worse is that everywhere I go, all anyone wants to talk to me about is football.

Just recently, I was sitting down for a meal with Katie in a lovely restaurant, when our food arrived.

I was about to have my first mouthful when a bloke tapped

me on the shoulder and said: "Gazza, do you remember when you scored that goal in Euro '96?"

"Of course I fucking remember it," I said. "I was there!"

I was polite to him and that, but I have barely any desire to talk about football these days, it's too painful. The football bits in this book are hard enough for me to go over and I'd rather chat about other things – the laughs I had with the lads, as at least that's something I am still able to do.

I don't even watch the big games on the telly, as all it does is make me mad with jealousy. I consider myself one of the best football players to have walked this earth, and I will always be so proud of that but the end of my career was the start of a downward spiral, and a sadness that has remained with me to this day.

6

DEATH OF MY DAD, JOHN GASCOIGNE

I'D BEEN SCARED OF MY DAD DYING SINCE I was a little lad, so when it actually happened in 2018 it was a huge blow. A year earlier, he'd been diagnosed with lung cancer, but as I've already said, my dad was a hard bastard and he always bounced back, so we weren't too worried.

There's no denying it, back in the day, Dad had been a bit of a boozer and a smoker, but by the time of his diagnosis he was the picture of health. He didn't drink, he'd quit smoking, and he was an extremely fit and strong man.

A doctor told him: "Mr Gascoigne, you're in such good shape we'll be able to give you twice as much chemo as we'd normally give a man of your age. You have every chance of fighting this."

As a family, we were determined he was going to beat the cancer, and we pulled together, as the Gascoigne clan always do in times of trouble. Lindsay rang me up to give me the news and I said: "Right, we will get through this. We just need to be there for each other."

For six months, Dad was blasted with chemo, and by the end of the treatment his tumour had shrunk to such an extent we were told it shouldn't bother him again, but that he'd need regular check-ups.

Fast forward another six months and my poor dad went for a scan at the Queen Elizabeth Hospital, in Gateshead, where he discovered the tumour had come back.

"There's no need to panic," the doctor said. "It's only small. We'll give you a six-week course of radiotherapy and that should do the trick."

It was winter, the time of the year when cold and flu season is in full swing, and to our horror, Dad picked up a chest infection, which turned into pneumonia. The chemo and radiotherapy had battered his immune system, and his body struggled to fight it. He was hooked up to an intravenous drip in hospital as the medics battled to save his life.

But after a few days they admitted defeat.

"We're terribly sorry," the doctor said. "There's nothing more we can do."

Lindsay rang to give me the terrible news and I raced up to Gateshead as quickly as I could but by the time I arrived Dad had already slipped into a coma.

I sat next to him, held his hand and talked to him non-stop for about 12 hours.

"You're my hero," I told him, because he was. He was a hero to all us Gascoignes, the head of our family, and I knew life would never be the same again without him.

"I love you, Dad. Thank you for everything you've done for me. Thank you for that football. Thank you, so, so much," I said.

He didn't reply, but he kept squeezing my hand, so I knew he could hear me.

Dad died in my arms in the early hours of Friday February 9th – he was 72 years old.

The funeral was held at Saltwell Crematorium, in Gateshead, close to where we all lived before I became famous.

As the hearse neared the crem I acted on impulse, as I so often do, and asked the driver to stop, so I could get out and walk in front of the car. It felt like a fitting way to honour my dad, to lead him to his final resting place.

The funeral was beautiful – Carl, Lindsay, Anna and I all took turns to talk about Dad, and how much we'd loved him. The service was packed with hundreds of mourners, including Peter Beardsley, who'd become a good mate of Dad's over the years.

It was a traumatic time for all of us, partly because of the way it happened. We'd all expected Dad to recover from cancer. He'd been through so much in his life, he was a survivor, and the doctors had given us a lot of hope.

I was sober when my dad died, and I remained so throughout the funeral and the wake, where no-one would have blamed me if I'd decided to drown my sorrows. Instead, I had a game of pool with Peter Beardsley. Thank God I had a clear head, as in the terrible aftermath there was a lot to sort out. I wouldn't have been any help to my siblings if I'd allowed myself to fall apart.

My dad's favourite phrase was: "Son, you're a fucking idiot." He was right a lot of the time, but I knew he loved me. On the day of his funeral I wanted to make him proud, and looking back to that awful time, I hope that I did.

6
SURPRISE

PROLOGUE

SURPRISE – A brief, intense state that occurs when encountering a sudden, unexpected event or piece of information.

SURPRISE? WELL, I'VE HAD MY FAIR SHARE OF surprises over the years, many of them happening first thing in the morning. Opening my eyes, head pounding, engulfed by nausea, I reach for my phone. I can always tell how much carnage I have caused by the number of unanswered calls and texts on my mobile. With trepidation, I open the messages, to find out what I've done.

I got the biggest shock when I woke up to discover myself all over the news after I visited the scene of an armed stand-off between the police and a gunman called Raoul Moat. Fucking hell, that was some surprise.

A similar thing happened after I took it upon myself to

drive a double-decker bus round Marble Arch in London. I was stuck in traffic so I jumped out of the car, got on the bus, and managed to persuade the driver to let me sit behind the wheel. I had the entire bus of around 70 passengers singing Cliff Richard's 'We're all Going on a Summer Holiday', and it was a right laugh until an image of my dad came into my head. "If he finds out about this, he will go fucking off it," I thought. I brought the bus to a halt and went back to my hotel. I thought I'd got away with it until I turned the TV on to discover I was all over the news. Sure enough, my dad was on the phone within five minutes. "Son, you're a fucking idiot," he said. "Sorry, Dad," I replied. I think the driver got into trouble as well, which I felt bad about.

These days, it's still a surprise, a lovely surprise, to wake up and realise I am sober, and no booze has passed my lips the night before. There's nothing like the feeling of being able to remember exactly what I've been up to and knowing I haven't pissed anyone off. Or, even if I have pissed someone off, at least I have a memory of it.

Yes, being an alcoholic and a world class footballer has meant my life has been filled by surprise.

There have been many surprises on the pitch, over the years, as anything can happen during a game of football, but probably the biggest was when Vinnie Jones grabbed my balls during the Newcastle v Wimbledon match of 1988. No-one expects that. The worst thing about the ball grabbing, aside from the pain, was the shock of it. It came from nowhere, and I was absolutely blindsided.

In fact, when I look back, my whole fucking life has been somewhat of a surprise, to be honest – it's been absolutely mental – the things I have done and the people I've met. I've had the privilege of spending time with some of the most talented footballers on the globe, as well as all manner of celebrities, such as Robbie Williams, Rod Stewart and Liam Gallagher.

My favourite film is Ridley Scott's *Gladiator* – I love it so much I once watched it over and over again for 24-hours straight. The best bit, by a mile, is when Russell Crowe's Maximus yells at the crowd: "Are you not entertained? Are you not entertained? Is this not why you are here?"

I am an entertainer at heart, I was like that when I played football, and I am like that now, at my shows. And in entertainment, there's always an element of surprise.

I've always loved to surprise my family, friends and the fans with gifts, gestures and amazing football. But don't get me wrong, there have been plenty of nasty surprises as well, such as the time I gave my sister Lindsay a carton of maggots instead of a Chinese takeaway. The maggots went all over the place when she took off the lid to tuck in – but she saw the funny side, people usually do. I've played loads of disgusting jokes like that over the years.

One of my favourite things to do is to surprise people with presents, and the money I have been privileged enough to make. Over the years, I've had thousands of requests for cash from people in need, and I would help every single one of them if I could.

I've turned up at people's houses in the middle of the night, and surprised them with thousands of pounds. Today, one of my favourite things to do is walk round the streets of Bournemouth, handing out £20 notes and cigarettes to homeless people. The look of surprise on their faces when they realise they are being given cigs and cash by Gazza is class, absolutely class.

1

VINNIE JONES

IT'S 1988 AND I'M STILL A YOUNG PLAYER AT Newcastle United, where I'm starting to make a real name for myself. Bobby Robson has recently described me as a "little gem", which is a brilliant boost to my confidence. I'm only 20, and for the England manager to call me that – well, it's still one of the best things anyone has ever said about me.

I was getting lots of coverage in the papers as the young lad with the fancy moves, and I suppose I was one of Newcastle's most well known players at that time. It hadn't happened yet, but later that year, Tottenham Hotspur would sign me for £2.2million, the most a British club had ever paid for a player.

It was February and we were set to play Wimbledon, which had a reputation as being a tough team with some hard players. The most notorious was midfielder Vinnie Jones, and I have to admit, I was pretty nervous ahead of the game at Plough Lane.

He was part of Wimbledon's so-called "Crazy Gang" along

with Dennis Wise and John Fashanu, all known for their aggressive tactics. I didn't know that much about Vinnie, but I'd seen him warming up, and the guy was fucking huge. "Oh, shit," I thought to myself.

As we waited in the tunnel, I had a good look at the man, and what I saw terrified me. I was a little fat bastard, but Vinnie? He had a skinhead, veins throbbing in his neck and his forearm was the size of my thigh.

I decided I had nothing to lose, so I went up to him and said: "Hi, Vinnie."

"It's just me and you today, you fat bastard," he spat.

Throughout the entire game he refused to leave me alone, and the first time I touched the ball he kicked me up in the air.

There was only about five minutes left when me and Vinnie were waiting for a player in front to take a free-kick. All of a sudden, out of nowhere, he stuck his hand out behind him, grabbed my balls and squeezed them hard. It was absolute agony and I screamed my head off.

We drew 0-0 and afterwards Vinnie came up to me and gave me a hug. "Sorry, Gazza, I had to do that," he said.

"Fucking hell," I replied. "You could have at least warned me!"

A fan had given me a bunch of red roses, and I got someone to take a single flower to the Wimbledon dressing room. I burst out laughing when Vinnie sent a toilet brush back.

I didn't think anyone had seen him attack me, because all the attention was focused on the free-kick which we weren't involved in, but the photographers had a field day.

In the images you can clearly see Vinnie's hand clamped around my balls, while my face is contorted in agony.

Those pictures went round the world, and the publicity we

got was insane. I still maintain I didn't need the press and it was Vinnie, as the lesser known player, who benefited from all that.

People continue to ask: "Did he really grab them?"

I just say: "Are you fucking kidding? Did you see my face? I was screaming!"

Vinnie and I eventually became good friends, and we'd go fishing together.

Katie has actually come up with a really good idea for a TV show – me and Vinnie Jones, travelling the world, learning about the rituals which surround death. The idea is that we will visit other countries together, and immerse ourselves in different cultures.

It will be brilliant if it comes off. Who'd have thought it, all these years later, exploring death with Vinnie Jones? Back then, I was just happy he hadn't killed me.

2

CHARITY

I CRIED AS I READ THE LETTER, FROM A DAD whose little girl was dying of cancer.

The fella, who was from Glasgow, had written: "Her final wish is to go to Florida, and swim with dolphins."

The problem was, I got so many of these letters, and there was no way to know if someone was taking the piss. My first instinct, always, is to help others, and that is something that has brought me no end of joy over the years – but I've made some silly mistakes in my time as well, and so now, I'm very careful about who I give my money to.

You know what I'm like, I get something into my head and I have the impulse to do it instantly, no matter the time of day. That's how I ended up driving to Glasgow in the middle of the night and knocking on this guy's door at 3am. He was understandably taken aback when he saw me standing there, on his doorstep.

"Can I see your daughter?" I asked him.

He went inside the house and carried his little daughter gently down the stairs and I could immediately tell she was in a bad way.

I handed him £15k there and then and said: "If you mention this to anyone, I want my money back. Go and enjoy yourself and let us know how you get on, maybe send me some pictures."

Another time, an elderly lady wrote to me while I was playing at Tottenham.

The letter read: "I have no money for Christmas – me and my daughter are starving. Paul, can you help us out?"

I did the same as I had in Glasgow – I went and knocked on her door to check she was genuine and I handed her an envelope containing £500.

"Have a lovely Christmas, darlin," I told her. "But don't tell anyone I have helped you. Keep it to yourself."

I was also incredibly moved by the story of a young girl in Sunderland, I think she was about 11, who had cancer. She'd had to have her leg amputated and she wrote to me saying: "I can't get to school."

I went out and bought her an electric scooter and told her: "There you go, I have a present for you. Get yourself to school, you've got no excuse now."

On one occasion I turned up at Bournemouth Hospital, unannounced, with as many toys as I could carry.

"Where's the children's department?" I asked the lady at the reception desk.

I was in and out of that kids ward as quick as anything, with no fuss. I left the toys, and then got out of there before anyone could take pictures, or tip off the press.

I was devastated when in 1996, while I was playing for Rangers and based in Scotland, gunman Thomas Hamilton went on the rampage at Dunblane Primary School, shooting 16 kids dead. He also killed a teacher and injured a further 15 children before turning the gun on himself.

Regan was a newborn baby, having arrived the month before, and I couldn't stop thinking about the tragedy of those innocent little lads and lasses, and the pain of their parents. I rang up Stirling Royal Infirmary and said: "Listen, it's Gazza. I am going to come down and see the kids. Keep it quiet."

When I arrived a little girl who'd lost her leg handed me a teddy.

"This is for your baby boy, Regan," she told me, and I couldn't help it, I just started crying my eyes out. There was building work going on at the hospital that day and one of the little boys covered his ears in panic at the noise, mistaking the sound of drilling for gunfire.

I felt so sorry for those kids, and I just hoped my presence helped in some way, at least showing them that I cared.

People don't realise as I have never spoken about it until now, but I've given at least £1million to charity over the years. I ring up the RSPCA and say: "Listen, it's Paul Gascoigne, here are my credit card details. If you tell anyone, I want my money back."

Like I mentioned before, one of my favourite things to do is to walk around Poole at 9pm on a Sunday, when everyone else is at home, handing cash, cigarettes and food to homeless people. "Don't say anything," I tell them, before immediately shooting off.

Anyone who knows me well will tell you I am a soft-hearted

bastard deep down. If I see someone in trouble, or in pain, I just want to make it better and being able to surprise those in need with help has given me a lot of pleasure over the years – it still does.

3

CELEB MATES & CAPERS

SITTING ON THE BALCONY OF MY ROOM AT the Chelsea Harbour Hotel in London, I gazed out over the marina, sipping on a glass of wine, thinking, 'this is the life'.

I was taking part in Soccer Aid 2006 and was enjoying some time on my own ahead of the game I was due to play in alongside some true legends and old mates including David Seaman, Les Ferdinand and Bryan Robson.

It was the first ever Soccer Aid charity match, held in aid of UNICEF and organised by Robbie Williams, and would see a bunch of celebs and ex footballers organise themselves into two teams, England and The Rest of the World, before battling it out on the pitch.

I was on the England team, managed by none other than Terry Venables, while greats such as David Ginola, Lothar Matthäus and Diego Maradona were our opponents. The game, played at Old Trafford in Manchester, was preceded by some smaller events, including a penalty shoot-out at Craven Cottage in Fulham.

I was taking some time to myself, unwinding on the balcony with a drink, when my phone began to ring.

"Hi Gazza, it's Robbie Williams," a voice said. "What are you up to?"

"Nothing. I am in bed, mate," I replied, worried he wanted me to go and train or take part in some other group activity I had no appetite for.

"No you're not," he shot back. "You're sitting on your balcony, looking across the water."

"Oh, fuck," I thought.

"I can see you," he said. "I'm in a room above you, to the left."

I had a look about, and sure enough, there was Robbie, standing on his own balcony, with a pair of fucking binoculars in his hands.

"Fucking hell, Gazza, what are you drinking?" he asked.

"A glass of wine," I replied.

"Come over here," he demanded. "Let's have a drink together."

So, I made my way across to Robbie's suite, where he was chilling out with his bodyguard, and we sat down and had a chat.

"What do you think of my new song, 'Rudebox'?" he asked me.

Well, it hadn't been released yet, and I'd never heard of it.

"Go on," I told him. "Sing it for me."

Robbie started to rap: "Ok then, back to basics, Grab your shell toes and your fat laces, A little hand clap for some funk faces, And make your body move in the following places."

When he'd finished he asked me: "Do you think it will do well?"

I hadn't understood a word of the lyrics, they sounded

absolutely mental to me, but I said: "Yeah, that will win, that will. Number one!"

When it was released later that year it was a bit of a flop in the UK, but it did reach the top of the charts in Italy, Germany and Switzerland, so I wasn't completely wrong.

Our conversation soon turned to a more serious subject.

"Are you fucking divorced now, Gazza? How much did you lose?" Robbie asked me.

"A canny bit of money," I told him. "Quite a bit, mate. Maybe more than three million."

"Ah, fucking hell," he said. "Just wait here, I'm going to the toilet."

When he came back he handed me a bit of paper and said: "Here's a present for you."

I looked at what he'd given me, and gasped when I realised it was a cheque for £3million.

"I can't accept that," I told him and though it pained me, I ripped it up into tiny pieces and put it in the bin.

"It's all right, Robbie," I said. "I don't need it."

Well, he got out his cheque book and wrote me another one, there and then, again, for three million quid.

"Please, Gazza," Robbie said. "Just take it and cash it in."

I just couldn't bring myself to do it, but I look back now and I wish I had just taken the fucking thing. I suppose it was pride that held me back.

It's not like Robbie couldn't afford it, he told me he'd made tens of millions from performing at Knebworth in Hertfordshire three years earlier, but I had too much dignity to accept his charity.

When we moved on to Manchester for the game, we had

rooms next to each other, and so we carried on drinking and having a laugh. The match was a lot of fun and England, captained by Robbie, beat The Rest of the World 2-1, after Les Ferdinand and Jonathan Wilkes scored goals. Robbie stole all the beer from my hotel room before he left, the bastard, but I didn't hold it against him.

A few months later, I was at my dad's house in Dunston when a big chauffeured car pulled up outside.

"Who the fuck's that for?" I thought.

A guy came to the door and said: "Gazza, Robbie Williams is in Blackpool. He wants to see you. I can take you there now."

"Ah, no, mate," I said. "I can't do that. I'm sober. Tell him I will come another day."

He's a good bloke, is Robbie Williams, so I knew he'd understand.

Another cracking lad I've had the honour of meeting is Prince William, who I sat close to at the England v Denmark game during the Euro 2020 tournament, which was actually held in 2021 due to the pandemic. I almost didn't make that game as I was drunk and I had fallen over and hit my head on a lamppost. It was quite a nasty cut, but Katie managed to patch me up, and we made our way to Wembley. Katie was sitting next to David Beckham, while Prince William was in the front with two bodyguards. I got an urge to say hello, so I clambered over some chairs, sat down in the seat next to him and gave him a kiss on the cheek.

"Gazza," he said. "What are you doing?"

"I don't know," I replied.

I was pretty drunk at the time, but I don't think he minded.

The next time I saw Prince William I was sober and he

seemed much happier to chat. It was two years later, and he was in Bournemouth opening a new branch of Pret a Manger.

"Gazza," he exclaimed when he saw me. "Is it actually you? What are you doing here?"

"I've come to see you," I told him, shaking his hand.

"How are you, are you OK? I'm keeping an eye on you from afar. It's good to see you," he said.

"I'm behaving myself now," I told him. "Cheers, Prince."

It was good to see him, and I was touched that he seemed genuinely concerned about me and interested in how I was. One of the good things about being famous is not having to introduce yourself or tell everybody your story over and over again. Every bugger I meet already knows who I am, which makes it easier to build up a rapport. It was that way when I met Liam Gallagher for the first time, in a restaurant in London in the 1990s.

I was in a taxi making my way back to Hertfordshire, when the driver passed the Groucho Club and said: "Paul, who do you think is inside there?"

"No idea," I replied.

"Liam Gallagher," he said.

"Stop the taxi," I demanded.

"Do you know him?" the driver asked.

"Nah, I've never met the fucker in my life," I replied. "I just have a feeling we'll get on."

I walked into the restaurant, quickly found Liam and said: "Hiya, nice to meet you."

"Hiya, Gazza," he replied. "Are you all right?"

I sat down next to him and he asked: "Do you want something to eat?"

"No, mate," I replied. "I'm not hungry, but I'll have a drink."

He went off to get me one, but while he was gone I started eyeing up his steak.

I couldn't resist it, I genuinely wasn't hungry, but I thought it would be the biggest laugh to gobble up his meal.

When he returned to the table he said: "Where's my steak?"

I looked him straight in the eye and replied: "I ate the c***."

"You fucking bastard," he spat.

"Two seconds," he said, and went away again.

I assumed he'd gone to get another steak but when he returned he was brandishing a fire extinguisher.

He absolutely mullered me with foam and I just sat there and took it – I knew I deserved everything I got.

When he'd finished I said: "See you later, mate." Then I scarpered.

I next saw him at a hotel near Loch Lomond in Scotland. He was sitting at the bar as I walked in and he greeted me like we were old friends.

"Are you coming to the concert tonight?" he asked me.

"What concert?" I asked.

"We're playing a gig at Balloch Castle Country Park," he said.

"I don't know," I replied.

"Come on, please, man. You'll love it," he told me.

"I tell you what, Liam, I'll do it, I will come and watch, but you have to put on a fucking display for me," I said.

"No problemo," he replied. "I will do."

Liam got me a limo to the venue, a beautiful castle with 200 acres of parkland on the edge of Lake Lomond.

I was in the middle of the audience and halfway through the set they shone a flash light on me. I was lit up for everyone to see, my face beamed onto huge screens next to the stage.

"Look who's watching us tonight," said Liam from the stage. "Someone who can drink more than fucking me."

"I have to show him a good time," he added.

Then, he said: "Gazza, do you want to roll with it?"

"Yes, mate!" I roared before he started belting out the famous tune.

I don't know what it is, but I seem to attract rock stars, for some reason, they can sniff me out from a mile away. I bumped into Rod Stewart once in London and he said to me: "Gazza, there's a pub down there, it's fucking brilliant, let's go."

"I'm desperate for a drink, Rod," I told him.

He pulled out a bottle of vodka from his pocket and handed it to me.

"I don't really drink vodka," I said, but took a large swig of it anyway.

When we got to the pub it was absolutely packed and I offered to go to the bar.

"I'm going to the toilet," said Rod.

I got the drinks in and was waiting for him to come back when all of a sudden I heard his voice. I looked around, and there he was, singing 'The First Cut is the Deepest' on the karaoke machine.

There was also the time in New York when I got pissed and fell down the stairs of the hotel I was staying in.

I was absolutely off my face and I must have tumbled down about 15 flights. Lying on the floor, unable to stand, someone picked me up. I opened my eyes, and to my shock and surprise, Phil Collins was standing there.

"You'll be all right, Gazza," he told me, and bought us some drinks.

We got on brilliantly, and he even gave me a pair of drumsticks as a gift. Phil and I kept in touch and sometimes I'd ring him up in Switzerland, where he lived with his wife Jill Tavelman.

One morning, I was a bit tipsy and decided to give him a call. Jill answered and I said: "Hiya, darlin', is Phil there?"

But she went absolutely off it with me.

"No, he's not!" she yelled down the phone. "Have you seen the papers?"

I was too pissed to have known, but the story of the day was all about how Phil was having an affair with Orianne Cevey, who would become his third wife.

I didn't call him again after that, I was too embarrassed.

Someone else's wife I have pissed off is David Beckham's – for some reason she thinks I am a bad influence on her clean-cut hubby. She's probably right, to be fair. Me and my dad went to stay with them once in Spain, when he played for Real Madrid, and I thought we had a lovely time. I've heard it said that Victoria, however, wasn't too keen on my antics.

I'll never forget David playing for England for the first time. It was 1996 and he was sitting at the front of the bus taking us to Moldova's national stadium for a World Cup qualifier.

I could tell he was really nervous and so I got hold of the mic next to the driver. I looked at David and I said: "Well, tell me what you want? What you really, really want?"

He just started laughing his head off and he played well in that game, which we won 3-0, so I credit myself with helping him to calm down. I really admire David for the way he's conducted himself, both as a player and as a businessman. He's done extremely well for himself and I am proud of him.

I'm terrible when I'm drunk, I call up all my old celeb mates, and pester them to death – Jamie Rednapp, Vinnie Jones, Rod Stewart, the lot. Someone I used to call all the time was Louis Walsh. I'd ring him, drunk, at 2am and sing Elvis Presley songs, then I'd joke: "Get us on *The X-Factor*, Louis."

"Gazza, would you fuck off?" he'd say. "It's the middle of the night and I'm in bed."

But I was relentless.

"Listen to this," I'd say, and start singing 'Wooden Heart', before, eventually, Louis would hang up, laughing his head off.

I am a massive Elvis fan and I've even got his autograph after my mam traded in an England shirt for it. When I was seven years old I won a dancing competition at school. The song I danced to was 'Jailhouse Rock'. My favourite Elvis song is probably 'Hound Dog', but I like all the fast ones. I don't like anything that's slow.

4

RAOUL MOAT

I CAREFULLY KNOCKED A HEAP OF COCAINE into a perfectly straight line, before snorting it through a rolled-up £20 note.

I was sitting in my flat in Jesmond, Newcastle, inhaling drugs and knocking back brandy, while the TV blared in the background. Needless to say, I was in a bad place at this time of my life, and it wouldn't be long before I left the North East for good, and moved to Bournemouth.

I often spent time alone, getting absolutely off my face on coke and booze. It's just what I did to kill the hours now I no longer had football, and to silence the terrible thoughts in my head. This was one such night, and nothing particularly out of the ordinary for me, but the difference was the country was in the grip of a huge breaking news story and it was happening on my doorstep.

A lad called Raoul Moat, a bouncer in Newcastle, who'd just

been released from prison, had gone on the run from police after a shooting spree. He'd shot dead his ex-girlfriend's new partner, Chris Brown, and blasted a copper in the face. The officer, PC David Rathband, was blinded in the attack, while Raoul's ex Samantha Stobbart, who he'd also shot, had survived.

I didn't really know any of this at the time, all I'd taken in was that this fella was now embroiled in a stand-off with police, who'd caught up with him in Rothbury, Northumberland, where I sometimes went fishing. It was the only news story on TV, which was broadcasting a picture of the guy, lying on his stomach with a sawn-off shotgun pointed at his own head, while a group of coppers angled rifles right back at him.

It was July 2010, and the whole country was transfixed by the developing story. By the time the cops had caught up with the man, he'd already been on the run for almost a week. The news channels were also running close-up pictures of his face and for some reason he looked incredibly familiar to me. I snorted another line of cocaine as I tried to work it out.

"I'm sure I know him," I thought to myself. It's possible I'd seen him around the city centre, where he had worked as a bouncer, but I didn't know this at the time.

"He's my mate, no doubt about it," I said out loud, as I prepared another line of coke to snort, riveted by the images of the stand-off on the TV screen.

Next, I gulped down what was possibly my 15th brandy, and I started to get it into my head this Raoul guy wasn't just my friend, he was my cousin.

"He needs my help," I thought to myself. "He must be cold, he must be hungry, he must really need a drink."

I snorted yet more cocaine, then went to see what I could

find in the flat which might be of use to a fugitive in the middle of a stand-off with armed police. I opened the fridge door and pulled out a cooked chicken and a can of lager. Then I grabbed one of my fishing rods, and a Barbour jacket.

"Right," I thought to myself. "I need to get to Rothbury."

Even in my drug-addled state, I knew no sane taxi driver would agree to take me to a police stand-off with a killer pointing a sawn-off shotgun to his head.

So instead, I asked to be driven to Newcastle Airport, which was on the way there.

"I'm going on holiday," I told the cabbie.

"That's nice," he replied.

By this point Raoul Moat wasn't my cousin anymore, he'd become my brother. Fuck it, he'd become my twin brother. As the taxi sped through the night, all I could think of was how I could relate to this guy. He'd lost his freedom and the love of his life, and now he was being hunted by the police. Well, the booze had often made me feel like a prisoner in my own home, Sheryl was long gone and I'd been hunted by the press, time and time again. Raoul Moat was my soul mate.

"I can help him," I told myself. "I've been in rehab. I'm a fucking great therapist."

As we came close to the airport, I ordered the driver to take a left, towards Rothbury.

"Where are you going, Gazza?" he asked. "Don't tell me you're heading to the stand-off."

"Yes, I am," I replied. "Raoul Moat's my brother, and he's cold and he's starving."

"Do you realise who he actually is?" the cabbie said.

"He's my fucking brother, I already told you!" I barked.

When we pulled up at the scene, it was like something out of Steven Spielberg's *E.T.* The place was crawling with police, and I was overwhelmed by the flashing lights.

I was completely spaced out and my first thought was: "There's a lot of people here, there must be a party going on."

I opened the door and climbed out of the car, being careful to gather up the chicken, coat, beer and fishing rod. The taxi fare came to £80, but the cabbie didn't even ask for it, he just sped off, clearly wanting to get the hell out of there as quickly as possible.

It wasn't long before I was approached by a police officer.

"Where are you off to, Gazza?" he asked.

"Raoul Moat's my brother," I told him. "I have some food for him, and a jacket, he must be cold."

"Are you aware he has a gun in his hand?" the copper said.

"Yeah," I replied. "But I can talk to him. I can get him to drop the weapon."

The police officer was unimpressed.

He looked at me coldly and said: "Pick up your things, the fishing rod, the chicken, and get out of here, quickly and quietly."

The copper didn't have to ask me twice, I gathered everything together, and started walking towards the nearest pub.

I'd probably snorted 14 lines of cocaine by this point, and downed God knows how many brandies, so I was in a right state, but despite this, deep down, I must have realised it would have been a bad idea to argue with the officer.

I made my way to the nearest pub and it was absolutely heaving with drinkers, while all the TVs in there were showing footage from the stand-off.

I ordered myself a brandy and started thinking about ordering a taxi when all of a sudden, out of the corner of my eye, I saw the words, "Gazza arrives in Rothbury to give Raoul Moat fishing rod and chicken", rolling across the bottom of a screen.

I was that out of it, I wasn't sure if I was imagining things, and I said to the guy next to me: "Is that me on telly?"

"Aye, Gazza," he replied. "You'd better fuck off."

I got a taxi home as quickly as I could and passed out in my flat.

I woke up the next morning, feeling like death warmed up, and with trepidation, I reached for my mobile phone.

"Oh, fuck," I thought to myself, as I saw I had around 300 missed calls, and 400 messages. When I'm drinking, I can always tell how much trouble I'm in by the number of people who've phoned and texted while I've been out of it.

Slowly, the drama of the night before came back to me, but it was hazy, to say the least. I remembered the flashing lights and seeing myself on the TV, standing there with a chicken and a fishing rod.

I switched on the television now, and learnt that Raoul Moat had shot himself dead overnight after a six-hour stand-off with police.

I now realised he wasn't my brother, he wasn't even my friend, and I just felt incredibly sad, both for him and the people he'd hurt. Picking up my phone again, I knew I needed to call my dad, who'd phoned me dozens of times.

"Dad," I said. "I am sorry. I did something wrong, didn't I?"

"Too fucking right, you did," he snapped. "Son, you're a fucking idiot."

"Oh, shit," I said.

The whole family was furious with me, but they were also

desperately worried. My dad insisted that I go to West Park Hospital, in Darlington, a mental health facility, where I sobered up very quickly. I didn't even take medication to detox, I just went cold turkey.

I was there for 11 days before my psychologist said it would be safe for me to leave. I went straight to my dad's house and apologised.

He was glad to see me sober, but he said: "You're a fucking idiot. Raoul Moat could have killed you."

When I look back, it's scary to think I did that. It was down to the cocaine, I never would have done it otherwise. I'm a lucky bastard, really, just to still be alive.

5

LIFE NOW

IT'S 5AM AND I AM IN BED AT KATIE'S HOUSE when I hear a knock at my door. I open my eyes and realise I'm sober, which is a surprising and joyful experience in itself, given the terror I often feel first thing in the morning when I am drinking.

"Come in," I say, yawning, and in walks little Nancie. The lass is just five, and she stands there holding out her right hand, saying: "Uncle Gazza, Uncle Gazza!"

I deposit a few Smarties into her palm, only for her to bleat: "More, more!"

I end up feeding her chocolate and wine gums non-stop as she keeps holding out her hand and I can't say no to her. I know Katie, her mam, won't be pleased when she finds out, but I can't help it. I love this girl, Nancie, like she's my own daughter and all I want is for her to become a mini Gazza, a proper little twat, just like me – I honestly believe she's halfway there already.

Nancie brings me a lot of joy, as does Katie and her little boy Mason, and I love to spend time with them at their house in Poole. I have my own place nearby, but I'll often stay in Katie's spare room as her family has become my family and I enjoy nothing better than being surrounded by them.

We do really ordinary things together, like go to the park or soft play, then out for some food.

We'll be ordering in a restaurant and the waiter will say to Katie: "And what does your dad want?"

I often get mistaken for her father, but I don't care – we think it's hilarious. For her birthday this year, as a joke, I bought her a card which read: "To my darling daughter."

The stupid thing is, Katie is the one who looks after me, not the other way around!

I love where I live, in Dorset, where I came 14 years ago to go to the rehab facility the Providence Project, in Bournemouth, which is brilliant and the cheapest in the country. But the first time I went, I didn't fully appreciate its value, and I quit after a few weeks.

"I'm going back up to Newcastle," I told my counsellor.

"You go home, and you'll be back within two days," he told me.

I didn't believe him, but sure enough, almost straight away, I was in trouble again.

A police officer discovered me drunk in a car, and the only thing that stopped me from getting into serious trouble was the fact I was in the passenger seat.

So, I came back down to Dorset, and did four weeks at the Providence Project that time. I knew that if I returned to Newcastle, I was in danger of also returning to my old ways, and so I decided to stay – but as summer became autumn, the temperature never once dipping below 20 degrees, I gradually began to fall in love with the place.

I got a house on Sandbanks, which is in Poole, close to Bournemouth, looking out across the English Channel, and though my heart will always be in the North East, I can't imagine living anywhere else now.

I haven't seen snow in the 14 years I've been here and to a North East fella like me, it feels as though I am living in Spain, or somewhere else abroad, not the UK.

I still pop into the Providence Project from time to time, to say hello to my old counsellors. I tell the patients: "If it works for me, it will work for you." But then I add: "Well, it works for me sometimes."

There's no point pretending I'm cured as I have now accepted I will always drink, I just try my best to stay sober for as long as I can, as often as I can.

It was while I was at the Providence Project that Terry Baker, my former agent, rang me up and said: "If you stay in the area, I can get you work, giving talks to fans. The money's decent."

It was the offer of work that cemented my decision to stay in Dorset and I found I enjoyed my "Evening with Paul Gascoigne" events.

"Gazza, Gazza, can I get a selfie?" I'm asked constantly before and after the shows. One night I didn't leave until 2am as I posed for more than 400 selfies – I thought my mouth would get stuck smiling, I was grinning that much.

But I'd do anything for the fans as to me they're not really fans, they're my family. Everyone thinks they're my fucking brother, and I love it. I feel as though they're my brothers too. Sometimes they cry, and often I join them.

As the lights in the theatre dim I am nervous to begin with, but when the audience begin to whoop, clap and shout my name and I realise how loved I am, I stop feeling anxious.

I tell all sorts of stories, mainly about my personal life and my drunken escapades, including the one I mentioned earlier, when I took a roast chicken to the gunman Raoul Moat because I'd become convinced he was my brother.

I hardly touch on football but I think that's why the fans love my shows so much. It's not just another evening with an ex-footballer; you get something different from me, I talk about all the mad stuff.

The events nearly always get sold out, and there can be as many as 2,000 fans in the audience, with some of them as mental as me.

When I played football, I loved to entertain the crowd, that was what gave me the buzz. I really miss that on a weekend, and the shows help fill the hole the game has left.

I'll never forget at one show, this guy said: "Gazza, can I have a selfie with you?"

"No problem, mate," I replied.

Then he added: "If I give you something, will you hold it?"

"Yes, pal," I told him.

Then, I watched in horror as he removed his glass eye and handed it to me.

"Would you pose with it?" he asked.

"Why not?" I said and did as he wanted, before watching as he popped the eye back into its socket. No wonder I have nightmares, fucking hell!

I'll typically do a long weekend of work every month, a couple of shows, an interview, and for the rest of the time I try to take it easy. When I'm fit enough, I love to be outdoors, going cycling, or fly fishing, and I like taking Katie with me, showing her the ropes – she had no idea how to cast a line before she met me, but now she's a pro.

I'm very settled in Poole, where everyone knows who I am and understands I can go off the rails from time to time. That can be annoying, but I also feel welcome, and as though I belong.

I was in my local Sainsbury's the other week doing a bit of shopping when a bloke fell on his knees in front of me and started crying.

"I love you, I love you so much," he said.

The guy had two young children with him and I just went: "Get the fuck up will you, your kids think I've hit you!"

The little ones were pointing at me and saying: "Who's he? Who's he?"

"Do you want a selfie, mate?" I asked the bloke, who was still in bits on the floor.

Eventually, he got up and we took a picture, and then he was on his way.

It's not too bad, the life I have created for myself in Poole, with Katie, her kids, my fishing and the beach.

It's taken some getting used to and it's come as a massive surprise to me, but I am learning how to appreciate the small joys, in exchange for the incredible highs and lows of my past. Today, the friendship of Katie, my sobriety and the enduring love of my fans, means the world to me.

7 FEAR

PROLOGUE

FEAR – A fundamental human emotion that serves as a protective, primal response to perceived danger or threat, whether real or imagined.

ON THE PITCH, I FELT NO FEAR. YOU LOOK AT some players and they're scared of the ball – as soon as they get it, they want rid of it straight away – but I was the opposite. I just loved to run with the ball at my feet and you need to be brave to do that, because it makes you a target. Defenders will try and break your legs, the crowd will give you loads of abuse if you lose it, not to mention your own teammates if they think you should have passed. Gary Lineker would tell me: "Gazza, the only time you ever pass to me is when I have no choice but to give the ball straight back to you."

But that was my strength – having the courage to do something different, try and make something happen. Bobby

Robson loved me for it, and he also knew I would never be bullied on the pitch – I was always able to handle myself and win any battle against my midfield opponent. You have to be strong physically and mentally when you're up against the most accomplished players in the world, and I'm proud that some of the best performances of my career came in the games which really mattered – in Italia '90 and Euro '96, especially.

I remember the build-up to the Scotland game at Euro '96. I was getting hammered in the papers after the dentist chair incident – they were calling me a "drunken oaf", a disgrace and saying I should be left out of the team. For most people, the pressure would have been too much, it would have affected their game, but I just wanted to get my own back.

"I'm going to score today," I told all the lads in the dressing room beforehand. "And when I do, make sure you come over, because we're going to do the dentist chair celebration." And when I did score – a wonder goal, no less – the feeling was amazing.

"Have some of that, you bastards," I thought, as I lay down on the pitch with my gob wide open. Alan Shearer, Steve McManaman and Jamie Redknapp were over quick as a flash with a bottle of liquid, which they squirted all over my face, as they laughed their heads off. Unfortunately it was Lucozade in that bottle, not whiskey, but it was a bloody wonderful celebration, one of my favourites. Even when all the players ran back to restart the game, I was still going crazy.

No matter how much people criticise me, they can't take away moments like that – moments I created myself, and which brought so much happiness and joy to the whole nation. Yes, I was definitely fearless on the pitch – I felt invincible, never inferior or scared or anxious in any way.

EIGHT

But outside of football, it was and still is another story.

My anxiety has always begun off the pitch, away from the 90-minute game, and is the source of much of my trouble. I have so many phobias I lose count – flying, the dark, dying, snakes, the number 13. You name it, I'm scared of it. If I'm honest, my fears often lead me to dark places and are part of the reason I drink in the way I do. All I want is to calm my nerves and quieten the voice in my head, telling me something terrible is about to happen.

1

FEAR OF FLYING

I WAS WEAVING MY WAY THROUGH THE terraced streets of Gateshead with my leather football, when my ears were filled with an almighty roar. I was familiar with the thunderous sound of the fans emanating from St James' Park on match days, but this noise was different. I looked upwards and saw an aeroplane flying low in the sky, so close I swore I could see the windows of the cockpit, and all of a sudden I was overcome with terror. Instinct took over and I dropped to the ground, arms over my head, as though this was wartime Britain and I was in the middle of a bomb raid.

I must have heard and seen planes above Gateshead before this, as it's on the flight path for Newcastle Airport, but this was the first time, around age seven, I remember being conscious of them.

From then on, whenever I heard the roar of a plane, I couldn't help it – I would be on the floor in nano-seconds, scared shitless, convinced it was about to drop from the sky and crush me to death. I'd stay planted to the ground until I could no longer hear the noise. I didn't know it at the time, but it was the start of a life-long terror of flying, which would eventually have me reaching for the bottle or avoiding the airport altogether.

It probably didn't help that my dad was also absolutely petrified of flying. When he worked in Germany he'd never fly, he'd get a ferry, and I think his fears must have rubbed off on me. My sister Lindsay is scared of flying as well. Going on holiday abroad as a family has always been a nightmare.

As a young player with Newcastle United I had no choice but to board multiple flights a year and so I was forced to find a way to cope, and I normally managed that by hiding a bit of booze in my pocket, which you could get away with in those days.

I actually can't remember much about my first ever flight but it would have been in May 1985, when Newcastle United travelled to New Zealand for a post-season tour. I must have been terrified, but I don't think the flight was as bad as I thought it would be.

I had my first proper drink on the return leg of that journey, which was a terrible experience for all of us. We had only been in the air for about five minutes when all of a sudden the plane plummeted at least 8,000ft, and all hell broke loose. Looking around I saw a bloke with his eyes screwed shut, mouthing the Lord's Prayer while fingering a wooden cross and just thought, fucking hell, my worst nightmare is coming true. The air hostesses were also panicking and some of them were even sobbing their hearts out.

I cried to the lads, "Give us a drink, guys," and I'll admit it, the way I got through that flight was to down whiskey after whiskey. I was so out of it, by the time I got to London my teammates had to bundle me onto a trolley. From then on, flying was hell for me and everyone around me.

I did have a few coping strategies that didn't involve alcohol, one of which was watching the air hostesses. If they looked relaxed, that helped, but if they seemed panicked, that would set me off big time. I'd also say the Lord's Prayer three times, and cross myself, even though I've never been religious. It was mad to be honest with you, but it calmed me down.

I know that part of the fear came from the lack of control I had over the situation and all sorts would be going through my head as the flight took off.

"How is the pilot, today?" I'd think to myself. "Is he happy, sad, angry? Has his wife cheated on him? What if she's had an affair and he's just found out about it? He's going to crash this fucking plane."

When I first started flying I'd often be able to persuade the pilot to let me sit with him in the cockpit. Getting to know the fella who held my life in his hands was a comfort, as long as he seemed like a decent sort, which he always did. They've stopped all that now, which is a shame.

I'd be as relaxed as anything, sitting in the cockpit, with my eyes on the pilot, able to reassure myself he wasn't hellbent on crashing the plane.

I felt so at home on one occasion, flying to Naples during Italia '90 ahead of our quarter-final match against Cameroon, I grabbed the controls and steered the plane off course.

We were about to start the descent when I said to the pilot: "How do you go right?"

He replied: "That small knob there, you turn it."

I asked: "Can I have a little go?"

He went: "Go on then, a tiny bit."

"Cheers," I said.

But I just couldn't resist. "Fuck it," I thought and started to steer the plane sharply to the right.

The rest of the team were in the back and I heard Chris Woods yell: "Get Gazza out of that fucking cockpit right now!"

I had one of my worst ever experiences while flying back from Arizona after being in rehab at Cottonwood Tucson, one of my favourite places to get sober. Having spent a month drying out, on that occasion I hadn't had a drink, and so I tried to distract myself by striking up conversation with the fella sitting next to me.

"Mate," I said. "I'm scared of flying. Really scared. Are you scared?"

Not a word from him.

"Did you hear me, fella?" I tried again but again, nothing but stony silence.

"How fucking ignorant," I thought to myself, as I went through my usual ritual of saying the Lord's Prayer three times, and doing the sign of the cross.

I turned to look at the guy again and that's when I realised there was something not quite right.

"He looks like a corpse," I thought to myself. I gave him a bit of a prod, and he didn't move a muscle. I collared an air hostess and said: "Darlin', I think there's something wrong with the guy next to me."

They found a doctor on board, who came and checked his pulse and confirmed he had died. The dead guy remained sitting next to me for that entire flight, and the air hostess put a blanket over him.

"Can I move to a different seat?" I asked her.

"Sorry, sir, there are no empty seats on the plane," she replied.

That's how I ended up sitting next to a dead person for nine hours, and falling off the wagon after spending a month in rehab. There was nothing else for it, I needed a drink to get through that flight, but what a waste of money that rehab was.

I'll never forget one of the first transatlantic flights I took, with my whole family, Jimmy and Sheryl – there were 12 of us altogether. It was just after I'd signed for Lazio in 1992 and I was treating everyone to a holiday of a lifetime at Disney World in Florida. We travelled first class and were in high spirits, looking forward to our trip, when all of a sudden the plane hit an air pocket and all hell broke loose. We all lifted out of our seats but Carl flew out of his and hit his head on the roof of the plane. We were screaming our heads off, convinced we were going to die.

My dad yelled: "I'm going to fucking kill that pilot!"

I avoid flying altogether these days, it's simply too traumatic. I would love to go on holiday, to Miami or somewhere else hot and glamorous, but the thought of stepping on a plane still petrifies me.

The last flight I got was from Newcastle to Southampton. I said: "Katie, I don't like this, I want to get the train."

"You'll be fine," she insisted. "It's only 45 minutes."

It was windy as fuck that day, and I just knew it was going to be a bumpy journey. Sure enough, the captain said: "Hold on tight. There's going to be turbulence as we land."

The plane almost touched down on its side, it was that bad.

"You cow," I said to Katie. "I'm never getting on a plane again."

2

FEAR OF THE LAW

IT'S CHRISTMAS DAY, BUT I AM SO OUT OF IT ON drugs and booze I have no idea what the date is. I'm turning my flat in Newcastle upside down, lifting up the cushions on the sofa, rifling through my bedsheets trying to find my mobile phone, but it's no use – it's lost.

The truth is, I've also lost my mind as I stagger the mile or so from my flat to Northumberland Street in the centre of Newcastle. I don't know what I am doing or what I am hoping to achieve as I stand there in the deserted shopping district, freezing my arse off.

"A pub," that's what I am thinking, as I lurch towards my favourite haunts, though any old dive will do, only to find every single one of them shut.

"What the fuck? It's daylight, isn't it? Why is everything closed? Where is everyone?" I ask myself, starting to feel paranoid. "Is this the end of the world or what?"

I find a phone box and ring 999, I don't know what else to do and in my opinion, this is an emergency.

"What service do you require?" the operator asks me.

"Police," I say.

They know me by now, the coppers. "What's the matter Gazza, where are you?" the officer asks.

"I'm on the high street, everything is shut. I need a drink, none of the pubs are open," I sob.

"It's Christmas Day, Gazza," the copper tells me.

They come and pick me up and they put me in a cell for six hours to dry out.

When it's time to let me go, the officer unlocking the cell turns to me and says: "Can I get an autograph, Gazza?"

"Fucking hell," I think to myself, but coppers are always doing this. Sometimes I wonder if they arrest me on purpose, just so they can take a fucking selfie.

In truth, the police have been all right with me over the years and I admit, I've caused them my fair share of bother. I've been picked up more times than I care to remember, put in a cell, and left to sober up. It's not the worst thing in the world.

The first time I got into trouble with the police, I was with Jimmy, who asked me to give some girls a lift home in my Mini.

"Nah, Jimmy," I said. "I thought we were going for a drink."

"We can go afterwards," he replied.

He managed to persuade me to do it, even though I hadn't got my licence yet, and I ended up knocking over this guy as he crossed the road in front of me.

I ran straight into the bloke because I hadn't seen him, and now he was lying there on the ground. I stopped the car, rushed over and I could see he was moving – I hadn't killed him at least.

But then I just panicked and drove off. I mustn't have been thinking straight, and was also terrified of getting into trouble with Newcastle United.

I know I shouldn't have done it, but I got a snooker cue and I smashed the windows of my car in, thinking I would pretend someone else had been driving it. Then I went over to my then-girlfriend Gail's house.

There was a knock on the door at 3am, and I just thought: "Oh, shit." Gail's dad answered it, and he said: "Paul, I think it's for you."

"It wasn't me," I told the police officer, but then I just started crying.

"How is he?" I asked. "Can I go and see him?"

"He'll live," the copper said. I'd been shitting myself that I'd killed him or something, so the relief was immense.

Jimmy and I had to go to court over that. We were fined and given points on our licence, even though I didn't have one yet. But the worst thing was I got a bollocking from Gordon McKeag, the Newcastle United chairman.

"If anything like this happens again, you're out," he told me.

These days, 90 per cent of the time, if I am in trouble with the police, it's because I'm drunk and they are looking after me.

Having said that, there have also been a fair few drink-driving and drunk and disorderly charges. I can't remember which ones led to convictions and which were dropped now. As I've already said, I no longer drive as I don't trust myself, it's simply not worth the risk.

The brush with the law which scared me the most happened in 2018 after I was accused of a truly terrible crime – sexual assault. I was travelling on the train from Birmingham, where

I'd been watching the boxing with my nephews, to Newcastle, and we'd gone past York, meaning we were nearly home.

We were minding our own business when two women started chatting to me, which is the kind of thing that happens all the time.

"Can we have a selfie?" one of them asked.

"Yeah, sure," I said, posing for a few pictures.

There was also another girl in our part of the train – I don't mean to be rude about her, but she was a pretty large lass and all of a sudden someone said: "You don't want a photo with her, Gazza. She's fucking fat and ugly."

Now, I've had my fair share of fat jibes throughout the years, from the fans as well as managers, and I know how horrible it can be. When I feel as though someone is being bullied, my instinct is to stick up for them, protect them. I will admit I perhaps didn't go about this in the right way, but I sat next to this woman, and gave her a peck on the mouth.

"You're not fat and ugly, darlin'," I said. "You're beautiful, inside and out."

She didn't whack me or seem angry, she just got off at her next stop, but a blonde girl on the train said: "You're going to get done for that. It's sexual assault."

I was shocked, thinking: "Sexual assault? How is that sexual assault?"

Later that day, the police rang me up at the Jesmond Dene Hotel, where I was staying while I was in Newcastle.

"I know what this is about," I told the copper. "I kissed a fat lass."

That perhaps wasn't the best thing to have said, but that's all that had happened – a quick peck on the mouth. Looking back, I shouldn't have done it, it was stupid of me, but I was just trying to make her feel better – I felt sorry for her.

It's fair to say, I was absolutely shitting myself when I was charged with sexual assault and had to stand trial at Teesside Crown Court. It didn't happen until the following year, which meant I had the case hanging over me for 14 months. For over a year, I was terrified I was going to end up a convicted sex offender. It sobered me up fast – I didn't touch a drop of alcohol for almost a year as it simply wasn't worth the risk. I knew that if I had to sign the sex offender's register, I was finished.

The trial lasted four days, and Katie was a tremendous support to me throughout that time. I don't know what I would have done without her. Each morning, I'd put on a suit and my sunglasses, and we'd walk into the court building in Middlesbrough town centre, side by side. The press were there every day, taking pictures of me, and I wanted to look smart – I was fighting for my reputation like never before.

Standing in the dock, I pulled out a montage of photographs of me kissing or being kissed by fans or celebrities including Princess Diana, Wayne Rooney, Ian Wright and Ally McCoist.

"Kissing is how I greet people," I told the court. "There was absolutely nothing sexual about it."

My friends and former boxers Ricky Hatton, God rest his soul, and Jane Couch both gave evidence, backing me up, telling the jury I am a naturally tactile person.

Even my old agent Mel told the court how I had once greeted a rabbi's wife by hugging and kissing her, not realising Orthodox Jews are forbidden from touching the opposite sex. It was embarrassing, hearing the evidence from the dock, but it was important for the jury to understand that behaving like an idiot doesn't make me a sex offender.

The prosecution tried to say I'd been drunk and slurring my words, which was a lie. Yes, I'd had a few drinks, but I'd just been fitted with dental implants and was finding it difficult to speak.

I hoped I'd done a decent job of defending myself, but standing in that dock waiting for the verdict was absolute torture.

As soon as the foreman said, "not guilty", I started crying my eyes out, I was so relieved.

"Thank you, thank you," I said. "I'd like to thank the judge, the jury – and my dentist."

I was referring to the implants, which meant I'd been slurring my words a little on the train, and everyone in the court burst out laughing.

"Are you all right?" Katie asked me as we left the building to a pack of photographers and reporters.

"Yes, darlin'," I said, as we smiled at each other. I stood with my head bowed slightly as my solicitor read out a statement to the waiting journalists, before joking: "Right, I am off to see my dentist now."

But in all seriousness, it was one of the scariest moments of my life, being accused of sexual assault. If I'd been found guilty, that would have been it, I would have been finished. I would never have worked again. I am so grateful to everyone who supported me during that difficult time and gave evidence in my defence. Without them, I would have been well and truly screwed.

3

FEAR OF DARK & DEATH

MY FEAR OF DEATH CAME TO ME IN MUCH THE
same way as my terror of flying – all at once while I was playing
football. I was in Saltwell Park, having a kick about on a crystal-
clear night, when for some reason I looked up at the sky. I was
seven, the same age I'd been when I developed a fear of planes,
and I'd never really noticed the stars before. There was hardly
any black for the trillions of bright specks, and for the first time
I began to really think about life, and my place in the universe.

"How long will those stars be there for?" I thought to myself.

Then, I began to wonder: "How long will I be here? What
will it feel like when I'm dead?"

Suddenly, a simple but certain truth dawned on me; when I'm
dead, I will never see my mam and dad again. I was overcome
with fear and I ran all the way home, screaming and crying. My
parents were in bed and I crawled in between them, holding on
to my mam like mad.

"What's wrong, son?" she asked.

"I don't know," I replied, the enormity of what had hit me somehow too scary and profound to put into words.

"You'll be all right," my mam said. "Just have a cup of tea."

She made me a cuppa and I fell into a deep sleep. It's funny, but to this day, if I am pissed and someone gives me a cup of tea, I'll fall asleep. I'm pretty much immune to sleeping tablets, they don't work for me anymore, but good, strong tea does the trick every time. Even when I was on cocaine many years ago, my mates at the time would be high as a kite, but I'd have a cup of tea and it would just knock me out.

The fear of death was really difficult to cope with as a lad. It would come over me all at once, the terrible realisation that one day I'd never play football again, never see my family again.

When little Steven Spraggon died in my arms it became much, much worse, and I developed the tics and twitches I have already mentioned.

I was also scared of the dark as a kid, which meant I couldn't get to sleep unless a light was on. All us kids were the same at home, the only difference was Anna, Carl and Lindsay grew out of it when they left, while I never did. I can't get to sleep now unless I have the television on, with the volume down. I know that if for some reason the TV switches itself off, that's it, I'll be wide awake and bolt upright in bed. It's weird, but I just put the TV back on again and I fall straight back to sleep.

Needless to say, I was a little anxious when Katie first floated the idea of taking part in reality TV show *Scared of the Dark*. I was told there would be eight of us, all celebrities, living in total darkness for eight days. During our time there we'd have to take part in challenges, but if it got too much all we had to do was shout, "I'm scared of the dark!" and we'd be able to leave.

"Fucking hell, Katie," I said. "I have claustrophobia, I'm scared of dying, I can't sleep unless there's a light on. Are you sure this is the right show for me?"

She managed to persuade me it was, but my family thought I was mad.

"Paul, you're shit-scared of the dark!" they all said. "What are you doing?"

We had a meeting first with a producer in a large room, and he turned the light off and said: "Let's see how you cope in the dark. Go and touch the wall over there."

Well, I stood up and ended up walking straight into a fucking cabinet. Anyway, despite that experience, for better or worse, I agreed to do it – my first reality TV series. Shown on Channel 4, *Scared of the Dark* was presented by Danny Dyer. I remember standing with him before I was due to enter the complex and saying: "Are we going to be all right in there?"

He just went: "I will, I'm not going in."

Then the lights went off, and I was so scared I was shaking. I walked in and my legs were trembling and the first thing I did was walk into a wall. "Fuck me," I said. "This, for eight days!"

I was the last celebrity in – Chris Eubank, Max George, Nicola Adams, Chris McCausland, Donna Preston and Chloe Burrows were already inside. Scarlett Moffatt came along a bit later. "Who's that, who's that?" they all asked, as no-one could see my face.

"Gazza," I said. "It's Gazza."

They all knew who I was, and I was greeted like a bit of a hero, so I felt a bit better after that.

I'd spoken to Chris Eubank before, at an awards ceremony shortly after the 1990 World Cup. I'd had a few whiskeys and I remember him saying to me: "Mr Gascoigne, I think you're drinking too much."

"Fucking hell, Chris," I told him. "I've just come back from the World Cup. You've only had one fight!"

So I wasn't too thrilled when I found myself sitting next to him. He's a bright lad, Chris, but fucking hell, he can talk, and he was the last person I wanted to be in there with.

"You're the King of England," he told me.

"Fucking hell, I'm not bothered," I said, trying to get my breath and calm my nerves.

He was always having a go at me, saying things like: "You're the king. The public love you, the country loves you, the world loves you, you don't need to be swearing in here."

I just said: "Do you know what, Chris, you could talk a fucking glass eye to sleep, you. Do us a favour, fuck off."

At one point I was telling the group the tale of how I'd sat next to a dead person for nine hours on that flight from Arizona after rehab. It's a bit disturbing that story, I admit, but it usually gets a few laughs when I recount it at my shows, and the other contestants thought it was hilarious. It definitely lightened the mood in that bunker.

That was until, at least, Chris opened his mouth and said: "Paul, stop talking so tragically about your life."

I have to say I was relieved to get away from him when he quit on day seven, but what I enjoyed most about *Scared of the Dark* was just sitting around and having a laugh with the other contestants. It reminded me of being a footballer, the times when we'd all be together ahead of a tournament. I don't like being on my own, and so it was great having the other celebs to chat with the whole time. I do get on well with people most of the time and I like to think there's not one person in this world I wouldn't be able to have a crack with, if it came to it. Even Chris Eubank is a good lad at heart, and I don't mind him really, he just did my nut in – calling me a king, and telling me not to swear.

I got used to the dark after a while, and I managed to work out where everything was. Chris McCausland, the blind comedian, really helped me with that, he was brilliant. He could work out where people were just by clapping his hands and feeling the vibrations, it was absolutely amazing.

I'd get lost trying to find the toilet and he'd say: "It's OK Gazza, it's just two doors along, feel your way."

On the last day, we had to vote for the person we wanted to win – I picked the amazing Chris McCausland – but I was the happiest man in the world when the other contestants chose me, crowning me champion of the series.

I was overcome with emotion and in tears when they announced it. I think people warmed to me because I was so open and honest about my own struggles. Danny Dyer switched the lights on in the bunker and I couldn't believe it when I saw how tiny the living space was. "How did I manage to get lost in here?" I thought.

I wouldn't want to be a blind man, fucking hell, but I'm perhaps a little less scared of the dark after that experience. It was my first reality TV show, and although I'd been terrified before I went in, I had a blast.

8
DISGUST

PROLOGUE

DISGUST – A feeling of intense dislike and revulsion in response to something offensive, distasteful or morally repugnant.

SOMETIMES I FEEL AS THOUGH MY WHOLE life is one vicious cycle of disgust which I haven't a hope in hell of breaking. Drinking in itself isn't the problem, it's the terrible aftermath and the consequences of boozing, which fill me with disgust. Waking up after a bender and reaching for my phone to discover I have hurt the people I love the most is devastating, and it's true – I feel completely disgusted with myself. The worst thing is, I have brought all this on myself and no-one is to blame but me.

When my calls go unanswered, which is understandable given I've behaved like a total arsehole, I know I deserve it. But then I get so low, I feel the only answer is to have another drink, and the cycle begins all over again. I absolutely hate it, but I can't seem to stop. The disgust is like petrol, fuelling my desire to carry on drinking.

Deep down, I would love to sober up for good but the thing is, I have tried absolutely everything, and nothing has worked. I have accepted it now – I will always be an alcoholic, which means I'll probably remain disgusted with myself for the rest of life – a difficult thing to admit.

I believe that alcoholism would have come for me in the end, no matter how my life had panned out. Sometimes people speculate I am the way I am because of football, but I know I would be in a much worse state without it.

I didn't ask to be an alcoholic but quite simply, I am one. The fact is, one drink is too many and 50 is not enough.

Sometimes I say to my family: "Why me? Why not one of you?" But there's no answer to that question.

I don't drink for the taste. You won't find me savouring a glass of wine, or an ice-cold beer, not anymore. I drink the drinks that clean you fucking out, straight away – gin and Disaronno are my favourites.

I could give you a million reasons why I drink, but my OCD is definitely one of them. I've driven myself to distraction with my numerous obsessions and the only thing which quietens my mind is booze. As soon as I sober up, the OCD comes back with a vengeance.

There are other addictions too. Fags – now, they're fairly harmless in the grand scheme of things and I only smoke about 20 a day. I have a couple of drags, and then I chuck them away. Crucially, cigarettes don't make me behave like a dickhead so I'm not too worried about them.

Believe it or not, Red Bull has also been a major addiction. Physically, I found it harder to detox from energy drinks than alcohol. At my worst, I was necking 50 of the twats a day, and the withdrawal symptoms were excruciating. Thankfully, I've managed to kick that habit for good, I only wish I could say the same for alcohol.

I was just a young lad and under a lot of pressure to lose weight when I first started making myself sick. I prided myself on laughing off the fat jibes, but I suppose they must have got to me deep down. When fans threw Mars Bars at me during games, I'd rip open the wrapper, and take a huge, dramatic bite – I thought it was hilarious. But staying in shape was a serious business, and I would have done anything to improve my chances on the pitch.

I suppose that's why I began to spew up. I'd be in the middle of eating something I absolutely loved – ice cream, for example – and then I'd suddenly think: "Fuck it, I may as well just make myself sick."

I'd really go for it then, and finish the entire tub, before sticking my fingers down my throat. I'd feel all right after that, start gobbling something else, and the cycle would start over again.

If I was enjoying a meal with family or friends, I'd join in with them, go to the toilet and spew up, then come back and carry on eating.

I got a fair bit of pleasure out of it and at the time it seemed like the perfect solution to my problems. It also gave me a buzz, but it was a stupid buzz, and I would feel repulsed with myself afterwards.

It was a horrible habit to have got into, and it filled me with disgust. The worst thing about it was I knew I was hurting myself and that's why, after five years of making myself sick, I decided to stop. I ended up with a stomach ulcer and I don't know for sure, but I feel fairly certain that it was caused by bulimia.

Something else which disgusts me is rubbish lying around, but that's the OCD talking. People can be messy, and I find that disgusting, to be honest with you, but I can't tell anyone what to do – no-one would listen anyway.

I also find it disgusting when people don't flush the toilet. It takes two seconds, why have a piss and then walk away? But that's minor when compared to booze, which is definitely the main source of my disgust. I wish it wasn't, but it is.

1

OCD

I'M SITTING IN MY HOUSE HAVING A CUP OF coffee, and I put the mug on the table in front of me. I notice its handle is at a right angle. I immediately begin to scan the room for other handles and I've got tunnel vision as I search for them. I feel anxious, as I realise the handle of the saucepan on the hob is at a left angle, while the handle of the kettle is pointing straight towards me. I'm pretty sure there are no more handles in view, but I start obsessing about the ones in the cupboards that I can't see.

"This is a fucking nightmare," I mutter to myself.

I walk over to the kettle and the saucepan and make sure the handles are pointing in the same direction as the one on my mug.

"That's better," I sigh, but then I notice a speck of fluff on the kitchen floor – and then another one. I bend over to pick them up and sit down to have a sip of my drink. But it never stops, this obsession of mine with being neat and tidy, and it's part of the reason I drink the way I do.

If you were to visit me at home, you'd see that my house is fucking spotless. I can't abide the tiniest spec of dust on a kitchen surface. I'm constantly cleaning, and it drives me crazy – this is the miserable reality of my OCD.

Drinking quietens the obsessions, but they hit me like a ton of bricks when I sober up – everything has to be perfect.

Like all kids at Christmas, Bianca, Regan and Mason would excitedly rip the wrapping paper from their presents and then discard it on the living room floor. That was an absolute nightmare for me, I'd have to pick it up and put it in the bin immediately. I'd miss out on their reactions and them playing with their toys, because I was so obsessed with the mess.

I'm not the only footballer with OCD, David Beckham has it too. He has to arrange items in even numbers, and keep everything in straight lines. I don't know whether it's OCD, but Steven Gerrard is obsessed with washing his hands – he does it 15 times a day – so at least I'm in good company.

I did once try and get professional help for my OCD, but it was fucking horrific, to be honest with you, and it didn't even work. Well, it might have helped a bit, but it certainly didn't make me completely better.

A therapist told me: "We aim to cure you through exposure. We'll prove to you there's nothing to be scared of. Mess, and your other obsessions, don't have the power to harm you."

"OK, I'll do it," I said, even though I was shitting myself.

One of my obsessions is with the number 13, I don't know why, all I know is that I fucking hate it. Every time I see that number written down, I look away and if someone says it out loud, I want to tell them to shut up.

If you ever want to get rid of me, repeat the word 13 over and over again, and you'll have me running for the hills. It's torture just writing this chapter, the number of times I've had to note it down already.

Anyway, this therapist hung a huge 13 on the wall of the room I was sleeping in.

It was the first thing I saw when I woke up in the morning, and the last image imprinted on my brain before I went to sleep at night.

He also called my mobile phone 13 times in a row, and sent me 13 text messages, then he left a load of rubbish on my bedroom floor.

"What the fuck are you doing that for?" I asked him.

"You'll get used to it," he told me. "It's not harming you."

I'd leave the room for a cup of tea, and I'd come back to find the therapist had moved everything around – what a bastard, it drove me crazy.

I always sleep on the right side of the bed, it's yet another one of my many obsessions.

"Sit on the left side, and talk to me," the therapist said.

"No," I said. "I am happy sitting here, thank you very much."

But he kept going on and on at me until I relented – it was torture.

I always put my right shoe on first, and then my left – it's a habit, an obsession, a compulsion, I can't help it. Anyway, you've guessed it, this therapist made me do it the other way round, and I freaked out so much I felt like chopping my fucking foot off.

All my coat hangers have to be neatly arranged and the clothes facing in the same direction. The therapist got up off the bed and opened the wardrobe doors.

"Where are you going?" I asked him.

"Nowhere," he replied.

"Get the fuck out of my wardrobe now," I told him.

Then, he started throwing the coat hangers all over the room.

"Fucking hell!" I yelled, feeling as though I wanted to scream, before picking every single one up off the floor and putting it back.

"Just leave them for a bit," he said.

Well, I was sweating, I was shaking and I wanted to kill the c***.

Next, he threw a bit of paper on the floor.

"What are you doing that for?" I cried.

"It's not harming anyone," he replied.

"It is me," I shot back. "I am picking it up."

"Go on then," he said.

I picked the paper up and put it in the bin.

"Does that feel good?" he asked.

"It does actually," I told him. "Cheers."

Then, the bastard picked it out of the bin, and threw it back on the floor.

By this stage, I'd had enough, and retreated to the bathroom a gibbering wreck.

While I was in there, I could hear him throwing all my stuff around.

I went back out and begged: "Please, can you just stop it!"

He gave me a break at that point, but not for long.

I also have a problem with plug socket switches. If I see one switched on with no plug in it, I have to turn it off immediately.

Well, this bastard made me go around the entire fucking building we were in, turning the switches on. It drove me nuts.

Then, he made me stand on the cracks in the pavement, which I've always avoided doing like the plague.

After a month of pure torture, I was absolutely fucked. I never finished the course of treatment.

I have to admit, I am a little bit better now. I used to get so upset by my obsessions I would be at the point of breaking down. Now, I just think, fucking hell, this again. I say the Lord's Prayer, cross myself and I walk away. It works most of the time, so I've found a way to cope with it, and at least my house is always clean.

2

DRINKING

I HAVEN'T SLEPT IN DAYS AND I AM LYING IN bed watching back-to-back episodes of *Paranormal* on BBC iPlayer. The fridge is stocked with fruit juice and water, my phone's on silent, and I know I just have to ride this out – that I will feel better eventually, as long as I don't cave and pick up an alcoholic drink.

I'm detoxing from a three-day bender, cold turkey. I don't take sleeping tablets or anything when I'm coming off booze, that feels too easy – I prefer it the hard way. I'm lucky I'm able to do it, to be honest, but it's what keeps me drinking, knowing I can stop when I need to.

I hole up in my flat, watch TV – *The FBI Files* is another favourite – down as much water as possible and wait. Needless to say, alcohol has caused me a lot of disgust over the years. Sadness and disgust are what led me to booze in the first place but I don't even enjoy it anymore. Drinking makes me disgusted with myself, more disgusted than I am when I am sober, but yet I still do it. How mad is that?

For years, I was able to drink like a relatively normal person. I mean, I am Gazza, I know I'm not normal, but booze was never a problem to begin with. I would have been about 17 when I had my first cocktail, a Pina Colada, in a nightclub in Newcastle. I absolutely loved the sweet taste of a Pina Colada, and I enjoyed beer as well. Nowadays, beer doesn't do a thing for me, nor does a Pina Colada. You may as well give me a shandy. No, these days, unless it's at least 30 per cent proof, I'm not bothered. I don't give a fuck what it is – if it's strong enough, I will drink it. But back then, I drank for the taste, and for the sheer pleasure of it.

I'll never forget being in Italy during the 1990 World Cup, drinking a Pina Colada in a little cocktail hut while the other lads were sunbathing. I'm from the North East, which means I don't sunbathe, so I was looking around, wondering what to do with myself, when I spotted this cocktail place on the beach.

"That will do me," I thought. "I'll have a Pina Colada please, mate," I told the barman. There was no-one else around, just the two of us, in this tiny hut in Cagliari, Sardinia, while the sun beat down on the crystal-clear Mediterranean ocean.

"This is the life," I thought to myself. "Here I am, on a beautiful island for the World Cup, sipping a Pina Colada, and no-one knows a thing about it."

But then, all of a sudden, out of nowhere, I heard a voice.

"Gazza, what have you got there?"

I turned round and my heart sank as I realised it was none other than Bobby Robson, manager of the England team, who'd already had a word and told me he'd be watching my every move to make sure I behaved. There was a strict no-drinking policy ahead of games.

"Strawberry milkshake, gaffer," I said.

"Can I have a taste?" Bobby asked. I properly shat myself then, but I had no choice but to offer him the drink, and wait.

"That's pretty good," he said, licking his lips. "Can I have one of these?" he asked the barman.

Thankfully, the barman was sharp and he'd cottoned on. To my relief, instead of giving Bobby a cocktail, he made him a milkshake. But then Bobby looked at me, frowning, and said: "Give us a taste of yours again?"

Nervously, I handed him my drink for the second time.

"This isn't the same," he said, looking confused.

The barman replied: "What do you mean?"

But Bobby just said: "Where is my umbrella and cherry?"

So I got away with that one, but only just. I also used to enjoy a really good bottle of wine, and even installed two wine cellars, one for red, the other for white, at my home in Kilbarchan, Renfrewshire, while I played at Rangers.

I remember, once, turning up at my favourite London restaurant, Le Pont de la Tour, pissed out of my brain. It was a fancy French place, and pricey as anything.

"Give us eight of your best wines," I said and they handed me a bill for £18k. In those days, I still cared what alcohol tasted like – now all I look at is the volume.

Despite what a lot of people may assume, there was never really a big drinking culture at any of the clubs I played for. I didn't really like socialising with the other lads anyway. I preferred the company of my old mates from home, and I was sober for most of the time and playing well. Of course, I'd have the odd binge and end up in the papers, but it was the exception to the general rule. I didn't drink much at all when I played for Lazio, or for Rangers. It was only when I moved to Middlesbrough in 1998 that alcohol became a real problem for me – but that didn't stop the papers portraying me in a bad light as far as booze was concerned, and sometimes unfairly.

Leaning over the snooker table, I took a shot before reaching for my bottle of beer and saying: "Your turn, Merse."

It was 1992 and it was a couple of days before the World Cup qualifier against Norway at Wembley. I was killing time with Paul Merson, who later became a teammate at Middlesbrough, in a London hotel ahead of the game. I'd been playing for England for four years by that point, but Merse was only a few games in. That night, he must have knocked back a pint of brandy and unbeknownst to me, he stuck it on my room tab.

I'd only had a few beers on that occasion, but Merse, who's since spoken publicly about his own struggles with alcohol, was in a bad way.

As always, England manager Graham Taylor checked the room bills to see what we had spent, and as well as the beers was the incriminating pint of brandy which I hadn't even touched. I felt totally betrayed when, without speaking to me first, Taylor told a press conference I had problems with "refuelling" in-between games, which was code for, I was drinking too much.

I could have dropped Merse in it, but I chose not to, and let everyone think the worst of me. He was having a tough time and I knew he'd be let go from the squad if Taylor found out. But it reflected badly on me, that, and more than 30 years later I've still not had an apology or thank you from that bastard Merse, though he's remained a mate to this day.

There were loads of times I was demonised in the press for being a drinker and often unfairly, in my opinion, but the truth was things didn't get really bad for me until the late 90s, when I hit rock bottom. I am an alcoholic, I know that now, and I think the booze would always have come for me in the end, even if I'd lived a different kind of life all together.

But as it happened, things started to get much worse where alcohol was concerned after the death of a close friend, David Cheek. Davey was Jimmy's cousin and we'd all grown up together. It was August 1998 and we'd gone out for drinks at the Dunston Excelsior, before getting some food at the Metrocentre in Gateshead, close to where I was staying at the Marriott Hotel. My dad and Lindsay were at the Excelsior with us, where we had a laugh and played a bit of pool, before me and the lads moved on to get some drinks and have an Italian meal – it was a great day.

But tragedy was to strike, and in the worst possible way. Davey, Jimmy and I all stayed at the hotel that night. At about 4am the next morning I got a phone call from Jimmy.

"Davey's dead," he told me.

I couldn't believe it. "What do you mean?" I asked him.

"He's not breathing, he must have died in his sleep," he replied.

I jumped out of bed and rushed down the stairs, only to see poor old Davey being bundled into an ambulance and driven away. I was absolutely devastated – Davey was only 43 and he had four bairns. He was a lovely bloke who would call me "The Boss" and to have lost him in such a way was heartbreaking for us all.

Of course, the papers had a field day, making a lot out of

the fact he'd been drinking with me on the night he died. A coroner later ruled Davey's death was the result of acute alcohol poisoning and that it was accidental – but the inquest also heard he'd suffered from heart problems in the past and that there was some evidence of natural disease. I guess we'll never know for sure why he died that night, or if it was only a matter of time before it happened anyway but it was difficult not to blame myself and I felt broken.

The funeral was terribly difficult for us all – Jimmy and I were pall bearers, which was a duty we carried out in tears, not caring who was there to witness our pain.

"It's not your fault," Lindsay told me.

I tried hard to believe her, but losing Davey in that way was too much for me to handle, and it led me to a dark place. I started drinking heavily, to the point of blacking out, which was terrifying.

1998 was also the year I missed out on playing in the World Cup, after Glenn Hoddle dropped me from the England squad at the eleventh hour. The two events had a catastrophic effect on me, and I began drinking myself to oblivion.

By October of that year, when all the Premier League clubs had a week off ahead of the Euro 2000 qualifier against Bulgaria, I was a mess. Hoddle hadn't picked me for that game, so I ended up going to Dublin for a four-day break with the Middlesbrough team. Having time on my hands was probably the worst thing that could have happened at that point. I was struggling to get any sleep, and taking a lot of sleeping pills, trying to blot out all the terrible things that had happened over the past couple of years.

For me, that break turned into a four-day bender. On the plane back from Dublin, I carried on drinking to calm my nerves due to my fear of flying, and that's when I started knocking back those hot toddies, all 36 of them. When I got to Newcastle, I somehow managed to get myself on a train to Stevenage, in Hertfordshire, as I was due to see my son Regan the following day, though I have no memory of any of this.

All I can recall is standing on the platform at Stevenage railway station, staring at the tracks in front of me, crying my eyes out, hellbent on jumping in front of the next train.

"I'm a total mess, a loser, Sheryl and Regan will be much better off without me in their lives," I told myself, over and over.

As fate would have it, a worker at the station spotted me and walked across.

"Are you OK, mate? What are you doing?" he asked, gently.

"I'm waiting for the next train," I sobbed. "I'm going to jump in front of it."

"The last train has already left the station," he told me.

"For fuck's sake," I thought to myself. "I even get it wrong when I am trying to kill myself."

I phoned Sheryl, beside myself, saying: "Please, please, help me, I don't know what to do. I just want to end it all."

She came and picked me up and took me to Hanbury Manor, where we'd got married in 1996, and I checked into a hotel room.

The next morning there was a knock at the door. I opened it and Bryan Robson, manager of Middlesbrough, was standing there.

"What the fuck are you doing here?" I asked him.

"Sheryl phoned me," he said.

Looking back, it was probably the best thing that could have happened, and I am grateful to Sheryl for letting him know what state I was in.

He drove me to the Marchwood Priory Hospital in Southampton, where I entered rehab for the first time.

Groggily opening my eyes four days later, I had absolutely no idea where I was or why.

"You're being treated for alcoholism and depression," a therapist told me. I'd been given pills to knock me out and had been placed on 24/7 suicide watch. Soon after I'd woken up, while I was still pretty dazed, I noticed another patient had come into my room.

"Get the fuck out of here," I barked, wanting to be on my own while I detoxed.

After I'd been in there for about a week, the guy came back.

One of the medics told me: "Paul, there is someone outside your room wanting to talk to you."

"I don't want to see anyone, I just want to be alone," I replied. "Tell them to fuck off, would you?"

I assumed it was a fan, desperate for an autograph, or to talk about football, the very last thing I wanted to do – but the therapist was insistent.

"He really wants to say hello," he pressed.

"No," I said. "Whoever he is, he can get the fuck out of here."

Again, the therapist said: "He's very keen for a chat."

Eventually, I relented, and said: "OK, then, let him in."

I couldn't believe my eyes when I looked up to see one of the biggest music legends of all time standing at the end of my bed – it was Eric Clapton.

"Oh fuck, hiya Eric," I managed to say. "I am sorry, mate."

Eric, who was facing his own battle with alcoholism, was

great and did his best to encourage me to stay, and keep me entertained.

He showed me his guitar and said: "You can have this, Gazza, if you do 28 days in here."

"OK, then," I replied. "I'll try."

In the end, I only managed to stay at the Priory for 20 days – just eight more and I would have got that guitar. I still think about it now, sometimes, but I was begging to be let out after three weeks, and I was unable to admit that I was an alcoholic.

I rang up Bryan Robson and said: "You need to get me out of here."

All I wanted to do was get back to playing for Middlesbrough.

I went to a few AA meetings after my stay at the Priory, but I didn't manage to keep it up and I was unable to stay sober for long. Even after the terrible episode at Stevenage, I still had a lot of fun while drinking, did mad stuff I wouldn't have contemplated sober, and much of it I don't regret at all.

There was the time, for example, I spent two days with a homeless person in New York. I checked into my hotel suite, which couldn't have been any more luxurious, with a beautiful en suite bathroom, and fully stocked minibar. I pulled back the thick velvet curtains and looked out onto the street below. On the other side of the road, I could see a homeless person, sitting on a cardboard box, swigging from a bottle hidden inside a paper bag.

By that point, I had become accustomed to staying in some of the most fancy hotels in the world. Don't get me wrong, I loved it, but there was no longer any novelty to it.

I spent a long time staring out of the window at that homeless person, just thinking: "What must it be like, to sleep in a cardboard box?"

Curiosity got the better of me and I ended up heading to a shop and buying some beer.

I walked over to the homeless guy and said: "Alreet mate? Would you like some cans?"

I sat down beside him and shared his cardboard box for two days, instead of sleeping in my five star hotel.

"I'm starving. Do you want a sandwich?" I asked him.

"Yes, please," he said. I went and got us two gigantic burgers then I put mine down on the top of a bin, thinking no one would touch it, while I nipped off to get another drink.

"Watch that burger for me, will you, mate," I told him.

But by the time I returned, he'd scoffed the lot, the bastard – two huge burgers – and that's when I left him, and went back to the hotel.

I was always doing mad stuff like that while I was drinking, just for a laugh, or to see what it was like.

Another time in San Francisco, I was boozing in a really rough Irish bar on my own when I saw two American guys laughing their heads off. I looked at them with envy, as that's all I wanted to be doing most of the time – drinking, and having a laugh with my mates.

I just went up to them, and I said: "Do you want to have a laugh with me today?"

They both said: "Yeah, OK."

I noticed they smelled terrible and so I took them to a shop, bought them brand new clothes, got them dressed, paid the bill, and then we had a brilliant day together, seeing the sights of San Francisco, and running around Fisherman's Wharf, which features in one of my favourite movies, *Godzilla*.

After I stopped playing football for good, I didn't give a fuck what anyone thought of me. It was a time for holidays and going out on the piss. I thought: "I have done my time. I have played football brilliantly for everyone for years, I have never let one team down, ever. It's finally my opportunity to go and have a brilliant fucking time."

And that's what I spent the following years doing. I travelled on my own, got pissed on my own, got myself into all kinds of trouble on my own. I'd end up in the papers and have to go and see my family and apologise for behaving like a daft shite.

I remember once, being at my dad's house, after I'd finished playing football.

"You're drinking too much, son," he told me.

"Oh, fuck off, Dad," I replied.

My dad was a hard bastard and he wasn't going to take that kind of talk sitting down, especially not in his own home.

"What did you say?" he demanded.

"I said, fuck off," I replied, slowly.

Two seconds later I was standing in his kitchen with blood pouring down my face, shaking with rage.

Something had snapped inside my dad that day, and he head-butted me in the face, bursting open my nose.

"I'm ringing the police," I told him.

How I had the nerve to ring the cops on my own dad, I'll never know.

"My dad's just beaten me up," I whined. "Can you come round? I'm bleeding."

Two officers turned up at the house, pushed me aside, and said to my dad: "Are you all right, Mr Gascoigne?"

"Bang that fucker up," he told them. "He's attacked me."

EIGHT

I was arrested and the police put me in a cell until 6am the next morning.

I woke up full of remorse, and headed straight back to my dad's house.

"I'm really sorry," I said. "I wasn't thinking straight."

"Don't be sorry," he said, handing me a bike. "Get on this fucker, and sober up."

"OK, Dad," I said.

I must have cycled about 30 miles on that bike, pissed as anything. I could have killed myself, I was so drunk, but that was my dad for you.

We loved each other fiercely, but he refused to ever take any shit from me.

I'd call him up drunk sometimes and head over to his house, only to find the door bolted and him refusing to let me in. I'd look down the street, to where Anna, Carl and my mam lived, and I'd see all their blinds twitching shut as he'd clearly rang up in advance, to warn them I was on the rampage.

Now, I am sober for the vast majority of the time, and I prefer it much better that way, but I still have relapses every few months.

I accept it's going to happen, and even plan for it, making sure my fridge is stocked up with soft drinks for when I decide to detox. It's not the drinking, it's the consequences, because I don't know when to stop. I only stop when I fucking collapse. There's no reason for my drinking, I just do it because I want to.

I've tried, I really have, to drink normally, but it's impossible – I am an all or nothing person. In 2018 I went to Australia and I had anti-alcohol pellets sewn into the lining of my stomach. It cost £20k and was supposed to give me the ability to enjoy a social drink, a glass of wine or beer, but make me sick if I touched spirits. It worked for about 18 months, I was capable of having just one or two, but it was miserable. It just made me feel awful the whole time and I decided I was better off without them – I'd rather not touch alcohol at all.

I used to drink for the most daft reasons. For example, if I had a potted plant in my house, and it stopped growing, I'd blame my drinking on that. I don't bother now, I just accept I am going to drink, no matter what.

Drinking used to be fun, but it's not anymore, it just makes me sad. Sitting in my flat, curtains drawn, entirely alone, I drink gin or Disaronno until I pass out. I never go out to drink in pubs or bars, and I don't think I have been clubbing in Bournemouth in 14 years.

If I drink, it's either in the house or in a hotel room, because it's easier that way, and I know I'm not going to end up in the papers.

If I am in a hotel, I can just ring room service, but when I'm at home, my OCD makes me think the place is a fucking mess and it takes me about three days to clean it all up.

I don't know how many tubes of toothpaste I use a week when I am drinking. I brush my teeth incessantly after every drink, and it gets tiring.

I admit I can still be a nuisance at times, especially to Katie, who often has to help me deal with the aftermath, but also the emergency services. On one occasion, I was sitting alone in my flat, head in my hands, miserable as anything and desperate to sober up.

I rang 999 and said: "Can I have an ambulance please, I'm really sick with the drink. I need to go on a drip."

I was taken to hospital and was checked in, but I got bored of waiting and so I jumped back in the ambulance and said: "Can you take me home, please?"

But once I was alone in my flat again, I totally forgot I'd been to hospital and rang 999 again.

"We've already come out to you tonight," the call handler told me.

"Oh, shit," I thought to myself. I have been fined a couple of times for wasting ambulance time, £260 or something, which is fair enough.

Luckily, I am able to bounce back from my drinking binges quickly enough, though it's taking a bit longer, the older I get – four days instead of three. I'm not a spring chicken anymore, but most of the time I make sure I am well enough to work, and Katie often can't believe it when she sees me.

"You were an absolute wreck last week," she'll tell me. "How have you turned it around so quickly, you look like a model!"

I have my face creams, face scrubs, and I just manage to get myself together, which is a good job, as I hate letting people down. There's also Botox, which I absolutely love. There's a guy in London who's a fan of mine, and he gives it to me for free. I've been getting it in my forehead for the last ten years or so. It makes me feel fresh. The only problem with Botox is it gets addictive after a while, like so many other things in life.

I just think, when I was younger, my parents told me what to do, then the teachers, then my managers. But I'm not young now, so no-one can tell me what to do. I know the best thing for everyone would be for me to stop drinking for good, and also that I would be happier if I did, but I have accepted now, that will never happen. Drinking fuels my sadness and my disgust, but it also numbs it, temporarily, at least, and that's what I need from time to time, oblivion, the ability to feel nothing, and I think I always will.

3

RED BULL

I WAS ONCE IN AN AA MEETING WITH A homeless bloke, a well-to-do middle-aged woman and a young lass, still in the detox stage, shaking like a leaf.

It's difficult to stand out at a meeting because sitting round the circle are people from all walks of life, some with even crazier stories than your own, united in just one thing – addiction.

That's the thing about alcohol, it doesn't discriminate. It doesn't care if you are rich, poor, young, old, nuts or sane. If it sets its sights on you, you've had it.

But that day, everyone was staring at me, because I'd done the near impossible – I was drawing the attention of everyone in that room. Eyes fixed upon the floor, I muttered the Lord's Prayer, not just once, but over and over again, like a madman. At the same time, I did the sign of the cross, repeatedly, as though I were possessed.

"Gazza, mate," said a pal I knew from the group, nudging me. "How many Red Bulls have you had today?"

I did a quick calculation in my head. There were the cans I'd had when I woke up, then again before and after training, three or four when I got home and another couple before I came to the meeting.

"Thirty, mate," I told him.

"Thirty?" he exclaimed.

"Yeah, thirty. At least," I replied.

"Fucking hell. I think you need some help, pal," he said.

"Help?" I replied.

"Yeah, help. To come off the Red Bull," he told me.

I realised he probably had a point as I felt absolutely horrendous. I wasn't sleeping, my anxiety was through the roof and my heart felt like it was trying to escape from my chest.

I'm not religious at all, but when I'm stressed, I cross myself, over and over. It's like a kind of tic I have, and related to my OCD. On this occasion I was going completely overboard with it. To look at me you'd think I was a devout Catholic, facing the noose.

My addiction to Red Bull had been creeping up over the years. I had started to feel tired before training, it was probably my age, and so I'd got into the habit of having a Red Bull to perk myself up. The problem was, I'd be double knackered afterwards, so I'd down another one to stop myself from crashing. It was a vicious cycle and the more I drank, the higher my tolerance became. It was like alcohol, all over again.

Things came to a head when I got myself a new car – a beautiful BMW X5 – in 2004.

I can't remember exactly what happened, but I was driving

somewhere in it and narrowly avoided crashing into a huge lorry, before I slammed into a van.

The air bag went off and hit me straight in the face, giving me a black eye, but to be honest I was lucky it wasn't any worse – I knew I had crashed because I was so jittery from the Red Bull. I went to hospital and they gave me one valium, to try and calm me down.

I laughed out loud and said: "One valium, what the fuck is that going to do? I've drunk about thirty cans of Red Bull today."

When I saw the state of my BMW X5, which was an absolute wreck, I was gutted.

"That's it," I thought to myself. "I'm going to have to go to rehab, get myself off the Red Bull for good."

I decided to go to Cottonwood, in Arizona, which as I mentioned, was one of my favourite places to get clean.

I checked myself in and they took my blood, gave me a once over.

"What are you in for?" the doctor asked. "There's no alcohol or drugs in your system."

"Red Bull," I replied. "You heard of it?"

"Yeah," he said. "How many cans?"

"Thirty," I replied. "Sometimes as many as fifty."

"OK," he said. "Let's find you a room to detox in."

"No way," I told him. "I don't want to be in a room, I'll climb the walls. I want to be outside."

I ended up sitting on a rock, in the middle of Arizona, for four days, barely moving in all that time. I looked up at the trees, and they morphed into crocodiles – fucking massive they were, like Godzillas.

I didn't sleep a wink while perched on that rock, heart hammering away in my chest. In fact, I didn't sleep for about six weeks while I was detoxing from Red Bull. I didn't want to take any meds, I just needed the caffeine and tourine out of my system, so I decided to go cold turkey and it was absolutely fucking horrific.

I was offered valium, but I knew if I took that, I'd go to sleep, wake up, and the Red Bull would still be there. So, I just sat on a rock and bided my time in the dry heat of Arizona, surrounded by tall cactus plants, willing the toxins out of my body.

All they did at Cottonwood was give me gallons of water to drink. They offered me food, but I didn't want it. At night, it would be 30 degrees outside, and I'd tip my head up to the sky, and watch the stars.

I was higher than a kite when I arrived, worse than when I'd been on cocaine, but I started to feel better after about four days.

In my experience, Red Bull is even more difficult to come off than alcohol. The withdrawal was excruciating, I was shaking like a madman. It was fucking dangerous, to be honest with you and coming off it was one of the hardest things I've ever had to do.

EPILOGUE

YOU MIGHT HAVE READ SOME WORRYING headlines about me, the summer before this book was released. *The Sun* newspaper published a dramatic story about how I was in intensive care after being found semi-conscious in my bathroom. None of it was untrue, but it made the situation sound much more serious than it actually was.

What a lot of people don't realise is that I suffer from a health condition called a hiatus hernia. It's actually quite common, and means part of my stomach bulges up into my chest. Sounds nice, doesn't it?

It causes some unpleasant symptoms, such as acid reflux, which burns my throat like a bastard and makes it difficult to eat.

Ordinarily speaking, I have a pretty decent diet, and I eat well. I have a fear of becoming yet another fat ex-footballer, so I try to look after myself and make healthy choices. I'll have a bit of grilled turkey, nothing too calorific.

But when my hernia is playing up, I really struggle to swallow and I'll be honest, drinking makes it worse. It exacerbates the condition and also stops my medication from working. There are periods when I stop eating completely, and I become malnourished.

The truth is, I've been going through a bit of a difficult time this summer as I've had a few relapses and the alcohol has made me quite unwell. When I'm working I force myself to stay sober as, believe it or not, I take my responsibilities seriously. It's when I'm on a break, or having a holiday, that I'm much more likely to pick up a drink, so summer is always a difficult time for me.

In July, I was in my flat in Poole, which I hadn't left in days, when my good mate Steve 'Fozzy' Foster found me in a bad way. I'll admit, I'd been drinking, and I'm not sure what would have happened if he hadn't arrived. I ended up spending a week in Poole Hospital so the doctors could treat my condition and get some fluids and nutrients into me. It was bad, but not as serious as the papers made out. I wasn't even blue-lighted to the hospital, Fozzy drove me there himself.

I'm feeling much better now and I am glad I've recovered in time to release this book. I'm living a quiet life at the moment, and spending a lot of time at home. I might go out in the morning, run a few errands, but then I'll just come back to the flat and chill out.

I'm not proud of myself for drinking this summer as it's caused me to lash out at the people I love the most and it happened while I was bang in the middle of writing this book, which I really wanted to finish.

I'm glad I managed to do that in the end, and to share this most open and honest account of my life so far. I'm far from perfect, but then who is?

Paul Gascoigne,
September 2025

ACKNOWLEDGEMENTS

FIRST AND FOREMOST, I'D LIKE TO THANK Katie Davies, my agent and friend. Thank you for your unwavering loyalty and companionship. Without you, I'd be lost.

I would never have been able to complete this book without the help of Victoria Williams. Thank you for listening, and for turning our conversations into the story of my life.

Thank you to Clare Fitzsimons, Fergus McKenna, Simon Monk, Christine Costello and Claire Brown at Reach for their hard work and dedication in publishing this book.

I also owe a huge debt to literary agent Oscar Janson-Smith. Thank you for your faith in the project, and for bringing Eight to fruition.

Finally, thanks to my brilliant sister Lindsay Gascoigne, for delving into our family history, and for standing by me, no matter what. I love you.